COMPLETELY IN BLUE

COMPLETELY IN BLUE

DISPATCHES FROM THE EDGE OF INSANITY

A MEMOIR

CHRIS CURRY

POST MORTEM PRESS
CINCINNATI

Cover design inspired by Jes Roy

Edited by Felicia Tiller-Sullivan

Post Mortem Press - Cincinnati, OH
Independent Press / Outside the Lines
www.postmortem-press.com

All names in this book have been changed except for when the specific person has granted permission for the use of their first name.

Printed in the United States of America

ISBN: 978-0615562865

To my mother and father. I can never thank you enough for everything you have done for me. And to my therapist, the late Teresa Sullivan, who taught me how to take control of my thoughts, in order to take control of my life.

FOREWORD

Greetings, reader! I hope you have some time available because the book you have picked up is one that you will not want to put down. Completely in Blue is a sometimes humorous, sometimes painful, but always hopeful account of the experiences of a young man battling mental illness. Chris Curry is brave to share his first-hand experience of the impact drug use can have on the human brain. He leads us on his trip to rock-bottom and his climb back towards the top.

At this point, you may be asking yourself if this book is for you. Let me assure you that it is! Whether you are a clinician, a student, a person with a loved one going through this, or are experiencing similar circumstances, this book will speak to you. Even if you have never had experience with this subject, I am confident that you will find something of value in these pages.

For clinicians, this book embodies the saying of Steven Covey, "Seek first to understand, then to be understood." This book helps us understand what our clients may be going through. By having this understanding, we are more apt to gain the trust of our clients. This improved relationship will enable you to assess and treat your clients more efficiently and effectively. Chris gives us the opportunity to learn about his feelings and develop empathy for his situation. He reminds us that our clients are humans first and patients second. Getting to know our clients' needs accurately will help us better identify ways to help them through the treatment process.

For students of the helping professions, this book is an excellent opportunity to try your hand at diagnosis and to develop your thoughts on treatment modalities. He experienced different diagnoses throughout his treatment. Like many patients, his experience was that his first one may not have been the most accurate. This is not that unusual an occurrence. As you read this book, you may want to consider what questions you would have asked in order to get a better understanding of his condition.

Keep in mind that building a relationship is very helpful in getting useful information, but this is a challenge in and of itself. Sometimes we do not have the luxury of having the time to develop these relationships, but our clients are very astute at knowing who is genuine and who is just there to get through the day. The more you can connect with your clients, the better your assessment will be. Take the time to see the person in your office as a person and not a patient. This will allow you to build a healthy therapeutic rapport with your client.

For individuals wondering how to help someone they care about, this book can help one recognize when someone needs outside intervention. Many times people care but do not know when or how to get involved. A person going through what Chris experienced is not able to make rational decisions, or they would not be making the choices they are. Help is not always easy to get. It may not have seemed so to Chris, but he was one of the lucky ones who got attention in a relatively quick fashion. If you think a loved one needs help, start asking questions NOW. Do not wait until things escalate out of control or it may be too late. There are steps you can take today, so there is no need to wait.

Educate yourself and become familiar with mental health services in your area. Talk to them. Even if your loved one won't accept the help right now, they will know that they can turn to you when they are ready.

For the person experiencing issues with substance misuse and/or mental illness, you may see a bit of yourself in this book. If you can see elements of yourself here, this book may help you find the courage to seek help. Many people who struggle with drug abuse are trying to treat an undiagnosed mental illness. If you find yourself in this book, I urge you to get help before it is too late. As I said before, Chris was one of the lucky ones. He was lucky not only because he got help promptly, but because he did not have to suffer the consequences that many face before getting treatment. He may not have felt that he needed treatment when he got it, but it was because of the treatment that he received that his life was turned around.

Chris has done more than share his experiences with us. He is also sharing his hope for the future. Chris is working to be able to give back to others. I believe that his experiences will continue to make him an asset to the helping community. We are lucky to have him!

Stephanie Beebe, MSW, LSW

1

Into the Barrel of a Gun

There's nothing in this world quite like staring down the barrel of a cop's gun.

Having him scream, gun drawn and pissed off, for you to 'Put your hands on your head and don't move or I'll shoot!' can be frightening for most people, but when you have already lost your mind completely, it's just another part of another day.

I felt as though I had just lost this one round. In fact, it took many years to fully come to understand all that I had lost, and many more after that to even begin getting it all back.

An hour earlier, I had escaped from psychiatric custody from the local medical hospital. The highly-secured psychiatric hospital in the city didn't have any beds available, so I was housed at the medical hospital with a 24-hour security guard by my side until one opened up. Since this was my third escape attempt, they were quickly coming to realize that a security guard just wasn't going to be enough to hold me.

The psychiatric resources back then were sparse, so keeping me at the medical hospital was their only choice; until I got into someone's home and went from being not only a threat to myself, but a threat to others as well.

Suddenly, the judicial and medical world started to perk up, coming to the realization that they had a major issue on their hands and that I needed to be completely and totally removed from society. There was a strange look of accomplishment on the faces of the officers who tracked me down that night as they hand-cuffed and leg-shackled me to the hospital bed. I wasn't going anywhere, so they could finally rest easy. Of course, that didn't stop me from using my only remaining weapon, my words, to let them know exactly what I thought of them.

I wasn't very impressed with the fact that the extreme force they had used to secure the handcuffs had left huge gashes on my wrists. I'm sure if they could have legally gagged me, they would have. Not only was I manic and not able to stop talking under the best of conditions, but after my capture, I was pissed off, violent, and hurling obscenities at the top of my lungs.

This was by far the best escape attempt yet. The first one wasn't really planned at all. I just sort of ran, and was quickly brought down by the ice in the parking lot and tackled by a group of security guards. The second attempt panned out even worse, though this one at least had some thought behind it, albeit psychotic thought, but thought nevertheless.

Out for a smoke break with my security guard, I had one of my visiting female friends chat him up in a flirtatious manner. As he was caught up in her fake interest, I slowly made my way towards the side of the smoking area, took a deep breath, and ran like the wind into the dead of winter. It was about 200 yards until I was off of hospital property, which was about as far as my limited attention span allowed me to plan then. I was so used to being caught in the first few seconds that it just didn't occur to me to think of what to do if I actually managed to make it off the property.

So I started running through backyards, which is no small task on a cold January night in two feet of snow. Once I got a few blocks down, I came out near the road and crouched behind a snow bank, slowly peering over to make sure there were no police cars about. I calmly walked to the first house I saw and knocked on the door. A middle-aged man answered the door and I fed him a line about being chased by a group of drug addicts who were trying to Bob me. If I could just come inside and call a cab, I would be ever so grateful.

He believed me at first, although I'm sure warning bells started going off when he realized that no matter what, I just couldn't stop talking. And not normal talking either; racing, jumbled speech that made sense only to me. I called a cab and waited anxiously, knowing that the police were out in full force trying to track me down. I knew the jig was up when the man yelled at me 'There's your fucking cab. Get the fuck out of my house.'

I looked outside and there were three police cars, lights blaring in the driveway. I admitted defeat and walked out the front door. The same police officer with whom I had been dealing on a near daily basis for the past three weeks was the one with his gun out. We'd had our share of run-ins on the 'outside' before they finally found a psychiatrist that I couldn't talk my way around, and had me committed. He had forcibly removed me from my old high school, the local newspaper office, the University residence, and a rundown hotel in the ghetto district. Every time he brought me to the ER in his cruiser, I would talk my way out of being committed and would be back on the streets, making his job difficult again the next night.

Drug-induced psychotic mania is an amazing thing. Up to a certain point, you can make anyone believe anything you want. Once you get past that point, however, there is no turning back, and it could take years for anyone to believe anything you ever say again.

For a while, I still had the wherewithal to pull it together enough when I was face to face with a psychiatrist. I knew the game, and I played it well. But once I had a gun pointed at my face, I had a pretty good feeling that the game was over. It turned out I was right, since that was the last time I breathed fresh air for over three months. I was shackled to the bed for a few hours, and then whisked off in a police car to the most secure psychiatric ward in the area.

Now, I was someone else's problem. And oh, what a problem I was. I wouldn't wish the job of the nurses, doctors, and orderlies that were assigned to my care on my worst enemy.

One of the psychiatrists at the medical hospital made the huge mistake of letting me know that no matter what I did, I could not be charged with a criminal offence. Since I was deemed as ‘posing a serious threat of bodily harm to himself or others’, and legally insane, the justice system just didn’t apply to me. If the police did charge me with something, it would immediately be thrown out, because I could not appreciate the consequences of my actions. It was well documented that I had been having frequent police-escorted emergency room encounters for quite some time. It was the worst thing he could have possibly said because I made sure to take full advantage of that clause to the bitter end while I was still free. And much, much more when I was finally locked up.

If that hadn’t been the case, I would likely still be in jail today, over ten years later. Attempted-murder, numerous assaults, assault with a weapon, mischief, theft, Robbery, drug-trafficking, evading arrest, inciting a riot… It would have been a considerable rap sheet, and a great portion of these charges would have been laid at the psychiatric hospital to which I was confined--at least the more serious ones of assault and attempted murder.

This whole scenario isn’t something that developed overnight. It was more like over a month. Scratch that. I guess if you want to get technical, it began many years prior, but for the sake of this particular story, let’s just go with a month.

I don’t suffer from schizophrenia or bipolar disorder. At most, I have some anxiety and intermittent depression, that I have been clear of for many years. But that certainly does not mean that I did not experience an extreme psychotic mental illness. Many years later, with the help of a wonderful therapist, I was able to understand how mind-bending drugs such as MDMA--street name Ecstasy--were able to warp my brain in such a way as to mimic major mental illness. The boundary between the sane and the insane is a very blurred one. I learned that even if you don’t suffer from schizophrenia or bipolar disorder and you do enough street drugs, don’t sleep for almost two weeks, and have an immense amount of stress, pretty much anyone can become psychotic. It doesn’t happen too often, which served to puzzle every single psychiatrist who was assigned to get inside my brain.

The terms 'bipolar' and 'schizophrenia' were touted about rather often. Psychiatric research and literature has come a long way since this experience, and now drug-induced psychosis is an official diagnostic label. But back then, they really had no idea what was going on with me. And even worse for me, they had no idea what to do with me, so they drugged me. Injections, pills, liquid medication…whatever was at their disposal. At the most severe point in my incarceration, there were 35 daily pills along with a daily long-lasting injection, the most powerful anti-psychotic, anti-depressant and anti-anxiety medication that was available at the time.

And the side effects of those legal drugs still remain today. The Tardive Dyskinesia has gotten much more tolerable and is now only noticeable to myself. The hair loss is something that I get to live with as a constant reminder of what I've been through. Tardive Dyskinesia is a condition caused by anti-psychotic medication that causes involuntary spasms and muscle twitches in the arms, legs and eyes.

Once the fog cleared, the TD certainly didn't make it very easy for me to integrate smoothly back into society. Even after I had regained my sanity, I appeared as someone who needed to be locked up, with my eyes constantly darting all over the place, my neck twitching involuntarily, and my arms moving on their own accord. It still acts up sometimes when I'm under great stress, yet it isn't something I worry about anymore. However, people still do accuse me of rolling my eyes at them, when in fact, I don't even notice I am doing anything out of the ordinary. It can create some unnecessary awkwardness in a conversation.

One of the many catalysts to this experience occurred one New Year's Eve: My introduction to ecstasy and the high-flying world of drug trafficking. It completely ruined every single thing about me in less than a month's time.

2

UNFATHOMABLE CONTENTMENT

New Year's Eve was sort of my time to shine in my younger years. It's the only day of the year where it is perfectly socially acceptable to get every single kind of fucked up, and no one bats an eye. I used to look forward to it, much as a child lies sleepless on Christmas Eve.

The night started out fairly normally at around six PM at a co-worker's apartment with a few cases of beer, all the hard liquor you could ever need and a few bags of weed. As I planned to maximize my New Year's to its fullest potential, this was just my starting point. I had two other engagements that I planned on attending as the evening wore on, and the ultimate goal was to end up with a certain someone as the clock struck midnight. That didn't quite pan out.

So after having a few drinks with some buddies and playing a few tunes on the guitar, I was ready for my next rendezvous. Thankfully it was only a few blocks away, as finding a cab on New Year's Eve is nearly impossible. So I trotted over to the home of another friend who was having a house party with a number of my other associates. I had never been to a party at Shane's place before, and I don't think I was completely prepared for the scene I was about to enter.

There were people on literally every square foot of the three level, four-bedroom house. There was a full-on techno dance party happening in the kitchen, a full-band jamming out in the basement and people everywhere. Literally, everywhere. I should have clued in that there was more than alcohol at play here, but I guess I figured techno-infused dance parties were just how some people liked to ring in the new year.

The main reason I was stopping at Shane's was to pick up some weed for my other friends who were waiting for me at another house party. That was my very close group of friends, including my band mates, and where I was supposed to be at midnight. So once I was able to drag Shane away from the flurry of drunk and high women throwing themselves at him, we went upstairs to his master bedroom. In hindsight, I should have also wondered how he could have afforded this lavish home on such a modest salary, though it didn't occur to me at the time.

We enter the bedroom, he locks the door. He takes out some sort of huge wooden chest and asks me how much I need. I think it was an ounce I was looking for, as I was buying for a few other people. So I paid him for the ounce and thought that our business was concluded.

"You sure you don't need any more?" he asked.

"Well, that's all the money I have on me, so yes, I guess I am sure," I replied.

"I could spot you if you want. That's no problem. How much do you think you could get rid of in a week?"

The answer that I chose to give to this question dictated how the next year or so of my life would pan out.

"Umm, I could probably get rid of a couple of ounces. What are you proposing?"

So we got to talking. I had sold pot a bit in high school, never in any copious amount, mostly to support my own smoking habit and nothing else. I doubt I ever had more than an ounce on me at a time. Shane proposed that he spot me a quarter-pound, so long as I could return the investment in a week. He gave me a great deal, which allowed for a huge profit margin on my end. As I had recently dropped out of college where I'd been studying journalism and was working a dismal call centre job that I despised, the prospect of making large amounts of money with little to no effort was thoroughly appealing.

The dollar signs were lighting up in my brain, and we had only just begun. For all the time I had known Shane, which admittedly wasn't all that long, I'd thought he just sold pot. And as any decent drug dealer would, that is the impression he purposely left until he trusted me enough to let me in a little further. Whether it was truly trust or just the fact that he was peeked out of his mind, I guess I will never know.

He opened another part of this wonderful chest of love, and took out a few vials of hash oil. Well, more than a few, actually. My eyes lit up, as the oil had always been my favourite cannabis product, but it was nearly impossible to find. So a few of these vials were added to my stash, with the fronted price that would surely allow me to make a mint on my investment.

Before I could even understand what was truly happening, another compartment was opened. "Think any of your friends at that other party would want some E?"

E is ecstasy. It creates a feeling of complete and utter euphoria in your mind and body. I knew my friends would be tickled pink if I were to show up with a few hits.

Being the professional drug peddler that he was, Shane didn't only have one kind. There were three: the purple ones were ten bucks, and they were relatively mild; a good starter pill. The blue ones were $20, and they would be a perfect addition to any moderately regular drug user's evening. The green ones were what caught my eye. He charged people $30 bucks a pill for these, and said he had never received any complaints. He was currently under the influence of one of them, and you could certainly tell that he was the happiest man on the planet.

We ironed out some prices, which once again allowed for a healthy profit on my part, so long as I could sell them for the allotted amount. He packed me up with a pretty little multi-coloured bag of happiness and sent me on my way. I had walked into his bedroom a simple pothead and left a full-fledged drug dealer. I had enough on me at that point to warrant some serious time in jail. We would likely be talking years. But of course, that thought never even crossed my mind.

Before I began my new career as a high-flying drug dealer, I had to sample the product. You know, just to be responsible. You have to know what you're selling people. It's just good business.

So I ground up some weed, laced some papers with hash oil and rolled a bunch of joints. It wasn't the cannabinoid-based treats that had piqued my interest, however. I knew what to expect from them. I had to try some of the rainbow.

Being the 'go big or go home' type back then when it came to drugs, I naturally opted for the green pill. I had plenty to spare, so long as I sold enough. I had ten of each kind, so thirty in total, along with a quarter pound of weed and ten five-gram vials of hash oil. I felt like a kid who had just Robbed a candy store.

I went downstairs to join the party and smoke a few joints with some friends. It couldn't have been more than ten minutes before it started. An overwhelming rush of pure contentment and joy. It was like my entire body was wrapped in an invisible duvet that hugged me gently no matter which way I moved. All of a sudden, all of the witty things that I think about when no one is around were actually coming out of my mouth in conversation. I was approaching women who were light years out of my league and holding my own. It was as though this feeling was what I had been looking for all my life. I wish it were a lie, but good, potent E is absolutely the best feeling in the entire world. I wasn't yet aware this was only the beginning. The good times were just getting started, and soon enough, I wouldn't even have to do the drug in order to get the effects.

Lost in my new world of unfathomable contentment, I quickly lost track of time. I was supposed to be across town at midnight to hook my friends up with some pot, and also maybe steal a kiss or two from the girl of my dreams. All of a sudden, that didn't seem to matter. Whatever I happened to be doing, was always the greatest thing in the world. I'm happy that Shane didn't own a dog, because I likely would have pet it to death. Every single thing I touched was amazing. Washing my hands became a life-altering experience. Every person I met was beautiful, fascinating and elegant, and everything I said seemed to have come out of the mouth of an accomplished scholar of the romantic arts. I'm not proud of this, but I even joined the techno dance party that was happening in the kitchen. It all made sense now: it's physically impossible to not dance on this drug.

Midnight rolled around and I realized that I had to get out of there, or I would have some very annoyed friends. For me, the night had only just begun. The place where I was going was the home of the guitar player in my band. All of our closest friends were there, and it would surely be a crazy scene until the wee hours of the morning. So, for this adventure, I figured that I might as well top up. I took another green one as I was lacing up my boots to trek into the frigid winter air.

The walk was fantastic. Even though everyone else was wrapped up in huge tuques and scarves, I had my jacket wide open. I wouldn't even doubt that I was skipping down the snow-draped road.

It was about a twenty minute walk, and in this cold winter night it felt like a fifteen second stroll on a California beach in July. I opened the door and immediately felt like Norm from *Cheers*. Well, Norm from *Cheers* if he was flying on two hits of ecstasy whenever he entered the bar. Everyone jumped up from whatever they were doing and greeted me at the door. There were hugs and high fives and kisses galore. They were all just drunk though. To me this was a much more intense experience. Human contact, of any kind, is a million times more enjoyable under the influence of ecstasy. I was just so damn happy to see them. Every last one of them. Even the few people there that I didn't know. Everyone was just great. I was in love. With everything.

3

OUT OF THE GHETTO AND INTO THE GUTTER

In order for the next sequence of events to make sense, some sort of context needs to be added to the story. The year prior to this fateful New Year's Eve had been a life-changing one on its own; and most certainly not in a good way.

Since writing had been in my blood for years, it seemed an apt choice to follow the family tree towards journalism school. So, at eighteen years old, I moved out on my own for the first time to an apartment downtown with a few friends from school. Since I was raised by an accomplished and respected journalist, who had actually taught the program years prior, I found that the course had little or nothing to offer me. I had already written for a number of newspapers in my young life; had even interviewed the Toronto Raptors NBA team on their views on racism for an article in a Toronto newspaper at the tender age of 13. So I guess you could say I felt ahead of the class, which made for the perfect excuse to ignore my professors in every way possible.

That first year of school turned into a party of epic proportions. What was once a nice hardwood-floored, spacious and beautiful two bedroom apartment quickly turned into the raunchiest, most disgusting party house that the city had ever witnessed. It probably didn't help matters that the liquor store was directly across the street. Whenever I woke up in the morning, or late afternoon, evening sometimes, the first thing I saw out the window was that gleaming sign, just calling my name.

I lived there for eight months; the entire school year. At one point, there were five of us living there, though anyone coming off the street would have guessed that there were at least fifteen full-time residents. If you stopped by on a Tuesday morning, you were sure to interrupt a ten person, five-foot bong session or an LSD-induced guitar jam. And the weekends were worse. Much, much worse. We became a frequent target of the police and had them visit us at least once a week. By the end of our time there, there was almost nothing left of the apartment. Everything in it had been sold to feed our various addictions, and everything that was a part of it had been destroyed by our ravaged lifestyle. And we had also been Robbed a few times during parties that got out of control. One night I recall, there was a line-up down the street to get into our apartment. It ended up in a huge brawl outside and many charges were laid. Thankfully, none of the charges were against us.

I wouldn't change a single thing about it if I could. I learned a heck of a lot about life, love, and loss in those eight months. Just after I moved in, I discovered that my long term girlfriend and high school sweetheart was having an affair with of my good friends, who happened to be a woman. After walking in on them together one day, the tides turned in my mind and a life of drug and booze-induced insanity seemed like the only way to escape the intensely traumatic emotional pain.

I discovered them one afternoon, and immediately vomited all over the hallway. I could smell it. I could smell the sex. It broke me. Completely.

This is the sort of emotional pain that an eighteen year old just doesn't have the life skills or even the mental capacity to comprehend. So, I chose to try to blur it away with drugs and booze. I held on, just barely, for a few months. But that was all I could muster.

I wanted to keep it together. It wasn't my plan to go to school and ruin my entire life. Once word of the girl I loved falling for a friend of mine came forth, there was no going back. I hit the bottle hard. I hit the acid hard. I hit the speed hard. I hit the weed hard. I hit everything; as hard as I could.

School became less of a priority and more of a nuisance; something that got in the way of me getting as massively fucked up as I possibly could every single day.

There were, of course, some great times. I still do know a few of the folks from 'The Ghetto' as we used to call it. It was a life-changing place for many people as it was the first place for us post-high-schoolers to go without feeling the wrath of our parents. It was great while we were living it, but if I had to go back there today, it would easily be classified as hell on Earth.

Like all great things, it abruptly came to an end. We had only leased the place for eight months and as school was ending, so was our time in The Ghetto. My one roommate, Kent, the guitar player in my band, had managed to keep a job throughout. He moved into a tiny apartment down the street that soon came to be known affectionately as 'The Asshole', as the space inside was comparable to such. I, however, did not work more than a few shifts washing dishes throughout those eight months and thus, had nowhere else to go except back to my parents' home in the country.

I had, somehow, managed to write a play in The Ghetto that was performed by the theater class at the school. It was called *Completely in Red*, and was written mostly by hand while I was high on Dexedrine and Adderall for about three days straight, in a room filled with people on various forms of stimulants and hallucinogens. I ended up getting screwed on that and only got paid in weed, so it didn't quite grant me the ability to take on the financial obligations of the apartment.

When I moved back home, my parents assuredly knew what was up, but that didn't stop me from lying my face off about everything and anything that had gone on during my first foray away from home.

My mother had actually stopped by the apartment one day after a 48-hour acid binge by my roommates and I. We were gone, having left the door unlocked for some reason. She apparently walked in to leave a note, but couldn't even find a clean spot on the floor or a table to leave it. Every wall in the entire place was riddled with acid-driven graffiti, booze bottles and pizza boxes littered the floor, and there was writing on every single wall in the entire apartment. I can't believe my poor mother didn't die right then and there. Though there was no point in even lying about what had happened there, because my parents full-well knew, I did it anyway. I was young and very, very stupid.

Once the letter from the college reached their hands, there was no way to lie myself out of the past eight months. I was not only kicked out of the journalism program, but I was banned from even applying at that school again for two years. These words were written very formally. Very formal, and very, very final.

Going from eight months of literal constant partying, to being isolated in the forest, 30-minutes away from the city, with your parents, who are extremely angry with you, is not an easy-adjustment. Things started to fall apart pretty quickly from there.

The horrible fiasco of my high school sweetheart becoming a lesbian with one of my best friends happened at the start of The Ghetto. So, around the four month point of the party, I was able to get into a relationship with someone whom I considered to be my saviour.

Every single little thing about her was amazing; she was perhaps the most beautiful girl I had ever known, she could party with the best of them, and she had the brains to go along with it. She was working part-time as a veterinary assistant and was also the manager of a lingerie shop in the mall while excelling in school. She was very driven for someone so young. Although it didn't last very long, it was a time that I will always remember. I was amazed with her, and about her. She was everything that I could have ever hoped for. But it turns out, that once you change the context, everything changes along with it.

Her name was Jennifer. After many months of me drunkenly trying to persuade her to be in a relationship with me, she finally conceded defeat and accepted me into her life. Once I was forced to move out of the city and back home, and without a car, things rapidly went to shit.

I was no longer the crazy party animal, musician, writer, and poet that she had grown to love. I had now become a defeated and depressed human being, stuck out in the forest with nothing to think about but my broken dreams. I had fucked everything up. Literally, everything. I was back at home, kicked out of school, no prospects, no future. Nothing to look forward to. Suicide rapidly became a reasonable escape option.

She stayed with me for many months after I went home. She tried. She really did. The times that we spent together became much less joyful for both of us. For me, it had become incredibly depressing and anxiety-provoking. For her, well, I can't even fathom.

I had lost something along the way. I wasn't the same person anymore. Life had suddenly thrown itself in front of me, and it was too much for me to bear. I fell into a deep and very, very dark depression.

My parents eventually let go of all the mistakes I had made in the past year, and even that didn't matter anymore. It wasn't them that I was trying to please. I knew that my life was on a dead track to nowhere, and it seemed as though there was nothing I could do about it. When at one point, our time together was filled with laughter, smoking joints during sex and random road trips to nowhere in particular, now I could no longer even muster the energy to speak. My words, not only to Jennifer—to everyone—began to disappear. I remember thinking constantly that I had nothing left to say. I had run my course; life was no longer worth living. There was nothing left to say. There was nothing left to say. Nothing. Left. To. Say.

I wrote the song *When the Fallen Soft as Herb* around this time, which is included in the audio accompaniment to this book, *Bohemian Cove: Completely in Blue*:

'When the fallen soft as herb
When the sweetest melody is heard
I would call you my friend true
I lay lost and broken, completely in blue.'

The song then goes on to speak of my realization of lying on train tracks to be the most effective and least painful means of committing suicide.

I had decided to die. And I had the perfect method. I was finally free.

She was terribly worried for me. I had gone from such an outgoing and loveable guy to a sad mess who could barely even string together the words 'I love you' any longer. Sex became mechanical and less spontaneous. I was living on a different planet than her. And on a different planet from everyone else in the world. I was going through what used to be known as a nervous breakdown. Now, the psychiatric literature would peg it as a major depressive episode.

I remember the day all too clearly when I had to call it quits. It wasn't because I didn't want to be with her, because I surely did. I wanted it more than anything in the world. I just didn't want her to have to witness my demise any longer. I was sitting outside my parents' house having a smoke. We were talking on the phone. After a lengthy pause that went on for much longer than is socially acceptable, I blurted out that 'I'm sorry, Jennifer. I just can't do this to you anymore. I love you, and I can't do this to you anymore. I'm so sorry.'

She knew exactly what I was talking about. She said ok, and we hung up. I sat in one spot for many hours after that, wishing I could cry. I couldn't. It was as if all emotion had been drained from me. All I knew was that she cared for me and that I could not let her go through seeing me like this any longer. I didn't want to lose her, as I loved her deeply, but I was so depressed that I could not even hold a conversation anymore. And it wasn't her fault, and wasn't something that I wanted her to deal with any longer. In the days after the conversation I wrote the song *Supermodel* which is now a staple of my musical project, *Bohemian Cove*. The chorus writes '*I'm so sorry I told you love you, it was all that I could say. I'm falling under, while falling for you, but I'm going away.*'

Never since have I written truer words.

4

SOAP AND TOWELS

Although that New Year's Eve eventually ended for everyone else in the world, it didn't for me. It sort of just never stopped. Well, I guess you could say it stopped when I was straight-jacketed and hand-cuffed, but that was well into February.

New Year's Day was when the downward spiral truly began. Throughout my time in The Ghetto, I had met many people who valued partying and hard drugs as much as I did, which made it easy to find people who would be willing to keep staying up and partying. My drug friends Paul and Doug had the ingenious idea to start snorting the E instead. This way, the effects would be immediate and, in theory, the product would last longer. So, that's what we spent the entire New Year's Day doing.

For most people who do E, there comes a point where you just can't do anymore. You need to take a break and sleep it off, perhaps even for days. Oddly enough, though, that never happened to me. Sleep was the last thing on my mind. It seemed like such a waste. I had a job to do.

Little did I know that my brain was changing in ways that would take years to undo, and would never be completely reversed.

There was a minor reality check when I realized that if I wanted to keep this up, I had better start moving some product. And since most of my friends were broke, I was going to have to be creative about finding prospective clients. I was able to sell a lot of pot and hash to my friends, mostly in small quantities. That just wasn't going to cut it. I had big plans for the crazy amounts of money that I was planning on making, and knew that I was going to have to go outside of my circle for this one. In addition, every time I went back to Shane's to give him a boatload of money, he always upped the ante and gave me even more product to push. Never one to shy away from a challenge, I always took whatever he was offering.

Although it's unfortunate to say, in my experience it has proven to be true: people who frequent strip clubs, as well as those who work there, buy a lot of drugs. So, that's where I went. I tried to treat it as a business venture as much as I could, and I was probably the best dressed drug dealer the place had ever seen.

I had an innovative approach too, and one that I'm sure not many other dealers have used in the past. Instead of paying for a lap dance, I would pay the dancers to go into the 'Champagne Room' and just talk. The looks on their faces when I told them that I didn't want a dance was always priceless and led to a lot of confusion. I just wanted to talk. I didn't want to grope them and drool all over them.

They spent all their time trying to please disgusting men, so I think they enjoyed the fact that they could just sit and shoot the shit with me. Within no time at all, I no longer needed to pay to get into the back rooms to talk to them. They had a crash pad above the strip club where they all hung out between sets, and within a day or so, I became a frequent fixture on the black leather couch. I think my kindness started to make more sense to them when they realized my ulterior motives of cashing in on the stripping industry.

It wasn't a huge place, so it didn't take me long to meet most of the girls who worked there. I discovered that the main drug supplier at the club came in the form of a prominent biker gang. This alone should have been more than enough to scare me off and send me quivering away with my tail between my legs, but it didn't. I was constantly flying on E every time I was there and the confidence was just dripping off of me. I knew that there was no chance that the bikers would catch on to me, so I had nothing to worry about.

I started selling weed, hash and E to nearly every girl who worked there, still, it wasn't quite enough. They mostly bought just for themselves and their friends, so it was a lot of work in order to make the kinds of money I wanted to make. I needed to become a supplier, not just a dealer. That seems to be the natural progression when it comes to drug peddling. Start off as a dealer, and then become the dealer to the dealers. You can't just look up drug dealers in the phone book, however. You have to find them organically.

One day when I was sitting in the strip club drinking a double rum and coke and watching one of my stripper pals, Stacey, do her thing to a song I had written and recorded, I spotted just the right person. His look just screamed drug dealer. He was in his early forties or so, had long scraggly hair, and wore a leather jacket and a bandana. I had seen him there before, so I pulled up a chair next to him and started making casual conversation. I had a method to figuring out people's stance on drugs that seemed to work well. I asked him if he wanted to smoke a joint and he most certainly did, so we got to talking. I told him of my connection for pot, hash oil, and E, and laid down some of the bulk prices for him. I was able to score a great deal from Shane, and my prices turned out to be a much better deal than he was currently paying. And, I was right; he was a dealer. A pretty damn big one too, as I would soon find out.

Normally, an accomplished dealer such as him wouldn't take too kindly to a stranger offering him a connection, but I have always been a pretty trustworthy seeming guy, and I had quite the confidence due to the amount of stimulants that I was constantly on, so it didn't take him long to feel comfortable.

We started out relatively small. I sold him an ounce of pot to begin with, as he just wanted a sample of the product to show his buddies. The stuff I was getting was by far the best in the city, so I figured that I had him hooked after that point. And I was right. We met again the next day, at the club, and started working on our business plan.

He wanted to meet my supplier, except I was a little too street smart for that. There was no way I was going to let him get to the source. He was my ticket to easy street, and there was no way in hell he was getting anywhere near Shane. So I fed him a line about Shane being overly paranoid and how I was the only person he would deal with, which worked. I kept him as my main client and main source of ridiculous income for the entire time I was on the outside.

He wasn't really interested in the E. He sold to an older crowd who weren't really into the designer drugs, though his pals loved the pot and the hash oil. After only a few days, I was selling him quarter pounds at a time. Steve and I became fast friends. I guess that's what happens when two strangers with similar goals meet and start making boatloads of money together.

During one of our exchanges of fistfuls of cash for copious amounts of dope, I happened to mention that I was a musician. Suddenly, his eyes lit up and he said 'well, I have someone that you have to meet.'

One of the buddies that he sold to happened to have a recording studio. One night, he brought me there. I think this is the point where I went from a simple hardcore drug user to someone teetering on the brink of insanity. It's really hard for me to tell at what point I crossed that border, but it must have been around that time. The reason it is so hard to tell, is that it took me many, many months to even come to terms with the fact that I had lost my mind. You would think that being locked in a highly secured psychiatric hospital would be enough to convince you, yet that was simply not the case.

I remember clearly the first time he brought me there. We walked into the garage and there was a group of guys in their late thirties to mid-forties sitting around drinking beer, smoking joints and puffing on cigarettes. They were all half-cut and immediately welcomed me into their circle with open arms. I guess Steve had already put in a good word for me. The fact that I was their drug supplier probably didn't hurt my chances of acceptance either.

Jamie was the guy who owned the place, a two-storey house, with a garage on the side. The studio was connected to the garage. When I walked in, he introduced me to the greatest fridge I had ever met. The only thing inside it was a keg of beer. This guy meant business when it came to drinking. There was a tap on the outside of the fridge, and I was given free rein to fill up my Mason jar whenever the urge struck. And I can assure you that the urge struck quite often. So the first night we all just sat around the garage, smoked weed, drank beer and shot the shit. I didn't want to impose, so I didn't even ask about this supposed recording studio. I had been burned in the past by people telling me they had a studio, when it turned out to only be a tiny four-track recorder in their bedroom. This guy seemed to have some cash, so I was eager to find out what he was hiding in the next room.

Once a few of the other guys left, Jamie decided it was time for the tour. I later learned that he didn't want many people in the studio, especially those who didn't play music. There were plenty of rowdy folks who hung out there, and he had no intention of risking the thousands of dollars of equipment inside. Cigarettes were not allowed in the studio. Beer wasn't even allowed; weed either. It now made perfect sense why everyone was hanging out in the garage.

I chugged my beer, butted out my smoke and he unlocked the door. I can still vividly recall every little thing about the studio. It was mind-blowing, to say the least.

You walk in and are immediately surrounded by a gigantic sound-proof jam room. There had to be at least five basses and fifteen guitars all hanging elegantly against the walls, along with the most elaborate drum set I had ever seen in my life. I had never been in a professional studio before, and learned then that this was called the tracking room.

Once I got my bearings in the tracking room and wiped the drool from my face, Jamie took me into the control room. Even though I didn't understand what most of the equipment in there was for, I knew that it was all worth much more than my life. We sat down in the control room and he blasted a few tunes that his band had recorded. The sound was just outstanding. Perfect in every single way. The musical ideas started firing through my brain immediately and wouldn't be hushed for many months.

He owned the studio but didn't do a lot of the recording himself, and instead had an engineer who came in to do that. Regrettably, he wasn't there that night, so we couldn't play around with the equipment and record the dozens of songs that I wanted to. He assured me that the engineer would be there the following night, and I was urged to come back and lay down some tracks.

Jamie was a bass player for the most part, and told me that he would do some bass for me and his buddy Rod would lay down some drums. Rod was there that night. He was certainly a cool cat. He looked like he had played in every single hair metal band that the eighties had ever given us, and he could drink and smoke with the best of them. It wasn't until I heard him behind the drum kit, playing my tunes, that I realized just how awesome this guy was.

It was probably two or three in the morning before I left the studio that night. I wasn't really living anywhere in particular then. My parents had moved into town by this point, but I had absolutely no interest in going there. They would not have taken too kindly to my current state of affairs.

I left the studio and went to my buddy Garvin's house. This came to be my crash pad up until I was locked up. Garvin had been a frequent visitor of The Ghetto and we became fast friends. His way of living was similar to mine during that period. He liked to drink, smoke and do drugs, and he lived with his dad who also enjoyed the same things. There was an open door policy there for his close friends, and there was always a couch available if need be. As our group of friends seemingly felt the need to nickname our party hangouts, his was called The Void. It's probably self-explanatory, but stepping into his house was like entering a void. Simple enough.

Garvin wasn't legally insane, but could have easily passed for such. He'd been raised in Las Vegas and went back there frequently, often for months at a time. His stories were stranger than fiction. But what made him even cooler was that he had a wicked speed connection. There are these two drugs named Dexedrine and Adderall that are used to treat people with Attention Deficit Hyper-Activity Disorder. In essence, all they are is speed. If you actually suffer from the disorder, the drugs serve to calm you down, allowing you to focus on the task at hand. If you don't have it, or if you do more than the recommended dose, it is quite simply the most potent form of speed that you can get. It wasn't legally prescribed in Canada, so Garvin imported his from the US. With my huge bags of weed, hash and ecstasy and his endless supply of speed, there was nothing that could stop us.

His place was where I went when there was no one else in the world who would be awake. You could always count on Garvin to not only be awake at 3AM, but to be ready to party. Somehow, he always managed to find like-minded friends who were up to the challenge as well. It didn't really matter what day or time that you got there. Even if he was sleeping, there was sure to be someone there ready to party.

So that night, Garvin and I did a bunch of speed, snorted some E and just talked about everything there is to possibly talk about in this entire world. Just doing drugs and talking wasn't ever enough for Garvin; he needed some sort of violence in his life. So we got into the liquor, and before you know it, he was practising his knife-throwing skills in his bedroom. Admittedly, he was pretty good, and could usually land it near the target. What irked me was that you never really knew when he was a certain kind of fucked up that could land the blade in your forehead. Garvin and I stayed up the whole night. A few other folks ended up stopping by at five or six in the morning, and pretty soon it was daylight. Time for me to shine.

I still technically had a job then, but you wouldn't know it to look at me. I hadn't shaved in quite some time, and my long hair helped me take on the hobo look fairly easily. I think I called in sick to work. Or maybe I didn't. Yeah, I probably didn't. I just decided not to show up. But in my defense, it didn't take drug-induced insanity to create that decision. I was working at a call centre that received in-bound phone calls for a cellular provider based in the US. It was a very sketchy cellular provider who took pride in screwing over their customers. The entire company was eventually brought down years later by a massive lawsuit on the part of their customers.

I worked in the billing department, for the company who constantly tried to screw their clients over on their bills. Your wildest dreams can't even imagine the degree of anger that was spewed towards me over the phone. And for the first time in months, I wasn't wickedly depressed, and the last place on Earth I wanted to go was to that hell-hole. After all, I was a high-flying drug dealer now. I didn't need their measly $12 an hour.

So I spent that day venturing around the city, just waiting for evening so I could get into the studio and lay down some havoc. I visited with friends, visited with people I didn't even really know and spent some time at some of the most dismal bars in the city selling drugs. I made my rounds, just counting down the seconds until Jamie was home from work and I could lay down some tracks.

When he returned home from his day job in the construction field, he found me on his front step. Waiting. I doubt he was too impressed by this, as he had a wife and kid, though he didn't let it show. His house was joined to the studio, but I never wanted to bother his wife or certainly his kid, so I just waited for him to come home to let me into the garage.

When we entered the studio, I immediately grabbed a mug and topped up from the keg. I grabbed an acoustic off the rack and started rehearsing what I was planning on playing. The ideas changed constantly. One second I wanted to do a certain song. Then it was quickly replaced by another. My attention span was that of a goldfish. The insanity had started to kick in. I hadn't slept in about four days, and had done enough E, speed, booze, hash and weed to take down any army.

Jamie popped his head into the garage and said he was going to have dinner with his family first and that Pat, the engineer, should be here soon. He would knock at the garage and I was to let him in.

While Jamie was inside with his family, I sat in the garage alone snorting E, smoking pot, drinking beer and smoking cigarettes. It was nearly an hour later that Pat showed up. I welcomed him in, as though I lived there, and explained that Jamie was having family time and would be with us shortly.

We talked about the project at hand. I just wanted to lay down some acoustic tracks for the time being. Pat wasn't as much of a partier as

Jamie was. He was certainly on the professional side of the music business, which was perfectly fine for me. Every single thing about him reminded me of Jack Endino. Jack Endino was a huge fixture in the grunge scene that developed in Washington in the mid '90's. He worked with Nirvana and Soundgarden. Although Pat probably wasn't consciously trying to play this part, I had made the connection in my mind. He even looked like Jack. Stunningly like him. And when he talked music, I felt like I was listening to someone who had been a fixture in the Seattle scene during the grunge explosion. I just couldn't wait for him to get behind the controls as I busted out a few tunes. He knew his stuff, very, very well. I still know him today and continue to respect him musically as much now as I did when I was insane.

Jamie eventually finished his dinner and joined us in the garage. He and I smoked a joint and I offered him a few hits of E. He was doing this for free, so I thought I should provide something. We threw back a few beers, smoked a joint and hit some E while Pat got the sound room all set up. It was only an acoustic recording, so it didn't take all that much preparation.

I didn't even show up at the studio with a guitar. I guess since I had seen the wall of guitars that were already there, it didn't seem important. My crappy acoustic wasn't going to do the trick. I knew Jamie would hook me up with a killer guit-box to record with, and he did.

We put out our joints and cigarettes and moved into the tracking room. There were about fifteen guitars in total, with about five acoustics in the mix that I could choose from. I didn't know a heck of a lot about guitars at this point, so I let him pick one out for me. I wish I could recall the make it was. All that I know is that it sounded fantastic.

Pat hooked the guitar up to the sound board and added about five room mics, as well as my main vocal mic. We did a few quick sound checks to make sure everything was picking up correctly. Once all was deemed a go, I started. I was too disorganized at that time to have any sort of track list. The insanity had just started to kick in and it was hard for me to keep focused on one thing for more than a few seconds. So I belted into some of my own tunes that I knew well.

There weren't even any second takes. I nailed every single one perfectly, the first time. It was as though I had been waiting my entire life for this opportunity to finally get my songs professionally recorded. It couldn't have been more than an hour and a half when we decided that we were done. We had eight songs. Both Pat and Jamie commented on how that was the quickest they had ever seen anyone record anything in their entire lives. Drug-induced insanity does have its perks, up to a certain point.

Jamie and I headed back to the garage to drink some more beer, smoke some more weed, and snort some more E. We left Pat in the control room to do some mixing to the tracks. He wasn't quite straight-cut, but compared to how I was then, he was a priest. And Jamie always liked to party. He worked hard and he played hard. That was his mantra.

After recording the eight songs in less than two hours, I was already on the ninth cloud. I hadn't even heard them yet but I knew they were golden. I knew that things were about to change for me. For the better, for once. I couldn't wait for Pat to be done so I could hear the results of the session.

It must have been about midnight when Pat came out of the control room and said that it was ready. My adrenaline, which was already off the charts, spiked again. Jamie, Pat and I went into the control room to listen. We closed all the doors, and Pat cranked up the recording as loud as it could go. The sound system in there was amazing to begin with, but hearing myself coming through the speakers was probably as close to a religious experience as I will ever fathom. I had never had much confidence in my song writing, or in anything else in my life up to now. When I heard the crisp and perfect melodies enveloping the sound room I knew that something big was about to happen in my life. Naturally, I thought that that 'something big' would mean fame in some way. Little did I know that the 'something big' would instead mean going completely insane and being locked away from society for months on end.

The only recordings I had done by then had been on a tape cassette recorder. Needless to say, the quality wasn't very good. When I heard my own voice and my own guitar riffs on the songs that I had written, professionally recorded, I was brought to a new level of ecstasy. And of course, I was on ecstasy at the time, so it was fifteen times more intense than it should have been.

I wasn't the only one impressed. Jamie thought it was fantastic and unique stuff, and Pat thought the same. They quickly brought the mix down to another console and ripped it onto a CD. Jamie asked me what I wanted on the CD cover but I certainly had not thought this far ahead. He found an image of two acoustic guitars crossing at the necks, in an X pattern, and decided that would be the image for the CD cover. Before he burnt the final copy for me, we needed a title for the CD.

Completely messed out of my mind, I blurted out something to them about how impressed I was that the bathroom in the studio not only had soap to wash your hands with, but towels to dry them with. The CD wound up being called *Soap and Towels*.

It wasn't *Chris Curry: Soap and Towels,* though. I already had a name for what was to become of me: Caparosa. Little did I know that this fictional character would take on its own life, spanning the next ten years.

Caparosa: Soap and Towels. They gave me about twenty discs with this engraved. By the time we were done, it was way past two AM, so I took off, amid many, many thanks, CD's in hand, and just that much crazier.

I went to Garvin's. I didn't have much of a choice, really, as his was the only place that I could hang out and sell some drugs in order to pay for my own massive habit I had developed. We did some speed, snorted some E, drank some beers and I forced him to listen to the CD. Over and over and over. Although he was pretty into the hardcore punk scene, he liked what he heard. And by hardcore, I mean it. He was into Las Vegas punk bands that end up in jail after every show they played. So him liking my acoustic CD meant something. I was onto something here; it wasn't just me. That was all I needed to hear.

It's hard to give an event by event time reference for what I did after this. What I do know is that I was snorting E on a twice-hourly basis and hadn't slept in four days. All I can really know for sure is that this is where things started to go bad. Really, really, really bad.

There is a reason that there aren't many books published regarding personal experiences with mania. There is the wonderful piece of work by Dr. Kay Redfield Jameson called *An Unquiet Mind* as well as the astonishing *ElectRoboy* by Andy Behrman. But for the most part, anyone who goes through psychotic mania never really develops a thorough enough understanding of what happened to be able to put it into words. It's sort of like describing a dream. Unfortunately, the incredible highs of mania are, at least in my experience, immediately followed by the harrowing lows of depression. To put it bluntly, when you lose your mind completely, along with everything else in your life, it isn't usually something you want to keep reliving by writing about it.

I guess I was different that way. I knew that what I had experienced in these months needed to be told. But time and time again, I could never do it. It took eleven years of trial, trial, error and error, but finally, here we are.

5

THE BELLS OF MADNESS

Having a copy of the *Soap and Towels* CD worked to only further my insanity, and it happened very quickly. By that time, my drug habit had progressed to a point of no return.

I was not only peddling my drugs to friends and associates, but I was also peddling my music. Garvin had a CD burner, which was rare back then, so I made many, many copies. Every single person I met was given a copy. Sadly, this is not an exaggeration. The record store guy, the pizza guy, every reasonably attractive girl I happened to meet . . .

At some point during that period, I realized that I was currently homeless. Every time I spoke to my parents it ended up in a huge argument. I didn't realize it for what it was, but I was in the hypo-manic stage, which meant that I would be much more prone to argument, and defying anyone who didn't think as I did. And I probably never would have known this, had I not decided to pay something back to society, many years later, and go to school to work in the mental health field myself.

Living with my parents was not an option. I went there a few times to grab some things I needed, but other than that, I was on my own. On the streets. I knew I could at crash Garvin's whenever I needed, and I had many other friends who would offer their homes. For the time-being at least.

I don't think any of my friends really realized what was happening to me then. How could they? They did not have advanced mental health training. They knew I sold drugs and that I was very high much of the time, but they were certainly not trained to know that their good friend had lost his mind.

But I had the CD now. I felt this was all I needed in order to show the world that I was worthy of being world famous. So I brought it back to the strip club, and the girls loved it. I became friends with the DJ at the strip club and he played my CD often while the girls danced on stage. For someone on the brink of insanity, seeing some of the prettiest girls on the planet rip their clothes off to your music can be an intense experience.

There was one song in particular, *A Turtle's Day in the Park,* which is included in the audio accompaniment to this book. It wasn't about a turtle, or a park. Honestly, I'm not too sure where the title came from, since I was quite out of touch with reality, but it was a beautiful song. The verse crept up slowly, and the chorus had an eerie sense of writhing, yet melodic pain attached to it. With the studio magic that Pat had put to it, it made for the perfect track to strip to. It started slow, and creeped up throughout, exploding in madness and pure ecstasy.

It was after seeing my dancer friend Stacey strip to my song that night that I could no longer look at her in the same way. I think the amount of songwriters who can say they have seen beautiful women take their clothes off as their song is played over the sound system could be counted on a few hands at most. Stacey and I became very close after this.

After that night, we hung around 'til closing time. The other girls went up to the crash pad but Stacey hung with me. We went to Shane's house after the club had closed. Shane was awake. Not only awake, but he was spun again. His roommate had just moved out, so he offered me the gigantic room downstairs to rent. Without even thinking about it, I accepted. Stacey and I went to scope out the new digs.

It was a huge room downstairs. For some reason it was furnished already. I don't think I even asked any questions. I just needed a place for the time being, and there couldn't be a better place to live than your drug dealer's house. So I gave Shane $500 for the month and I now had an official crash pad. He certainly did not mind me bringing strippers over to the house, and Stacey did not mind coming home after work to such a luxurious house, filled with free drugs and music.

At the time, I thought I was living the dream. I had just released a CD, I was dating a stripper and I had more drugs and money than I knew what to do with. Every single second of every single day was a party. It wasn't until I hung out with my real friends that I started to realize that something may be amiss.

Somehow, I had held on to a very responsible friend throughout. His name was Bryan and I knew him from high school. He was a very talented writer who had become passionately involved in Buddhism, and was very much at peace with himself and everyone around him, which is why I tried to avoid him during my times of insanity. But being the good friend that he was, he tracked me down and brought me to his house one night.

I thought he just wanted to hang out and drink some beers and smoke some weed, but, that was not the case. It was awkward from the time I got there. I was breaking out the joints and the bottles for a good night ahead, but he kept on telling me that we couldn't smoke the joints and that I should leave the bottles for another time.

Then the friend who played in my high school band showed up. I had ignored him for many months, because I knew he could not keep up with, or approve, of my new life of doing all the drugs that I could do. I was cornered.

It was an intervention. They didn't call it that, but that's what it was. They had both even spoken to my parents. My parents had asked them if they could please try to talk some sense into me, so Bryan cornered me in his house and did his best.

I was not yet psychotic, but I was ragingly manic. I could not sit down. At all. I needed to always be on my feet. He had a pool table, which kept my attention while he told me how worried he was about me.

He could have been telling me that the world was about to end, and it still wouldn't have phased me. I knew I was right, and they were wrong. I kept trying to pour a drink, and he would always take it away. At first, that was fine, but after about two hours of my friend taking away everything I wanted, shit got serious.

The thing with my experience with mania is that it can turn on a dime. One second, I'm the happiest person in the world but the moment that someone crosses my path, I want to kill them. We all smoked cigarettes, so we went outside for one. When I went to light a joint first, he grabbed it and threw it away. I lost it. I didn't get physically violent, but I was out of there. I stormed off down the street, incredibly angry and shouting of some perceived injustice that had been bestowed on me.

I didn't find out until months later that my mother had put him up to that intervention. She couldn't talk to me anymore, so she hoped that my closest friends could. But no, I blew them off too. It's a painful road to walk down once you regain some sense of reality.

6

The Medical and Legal Community vs. My Unbridled Insanity

My first of many encounters with the police was an interesting one. The weather had lightened up a bit for January and I was out on the town, probably with no real intentions. Since I was in a relatively small town, it wasn't out of the ordinary that I ran into my mother in my travels. She told me to get in the car, and I grudgingly acquiesced. She hadn't seen or heard from me in days. I hadn't shaved at all, and my hair was long and mangy, and I was talking a mile a minute.

She wanted me to come home, get some rest. I emphatically did not wish to do this. She started driving away with me in the car and I lost it. I screamed for her to let me out. When she didn't oblige, I opened the door of the moving car and jumped out. Although we were on a residential street and not going very fast, this was still a dangerous option, but the possibility of danger didn't really deter me from much back then.

I fell on the ground and immediately got up and ran off into some bushes. I needed to get away from my mother. She just didn't understand. She kept telling me I was 'sick' but how could I be sick when I had never felt better in my entire life? I likely thought that she was the one who was insane.

When I knew that I had successfully escaped my mother, I realized that I was near my old high school from which I had graduated the past year, and thus, still knew a few people. It was lunch time, so there were a bunch of people out in the smoking area. I knew if there was anyone that I knew there, they would certainly be found in the smoking section. And I was right. It was the perfect place for me. Since I couldn't stop talking, it was excellent to have an audience of intrigued teens hanging on my every word.

I regaled them with stories of my pending record contract (that existed solely in my mind) and told them how I had recently discovered that I had a genius IQ, which also had no basis in fact or reality. But it was true to me. And then, I decided that I should try to become the assistant principal of the high school. It seemed like a perfectly reasonable goal in my diseased mind.

During my time there, I had frequent run-ins with the assistant principal. He took it on himself to be the truancy police and I was often in his office. He once even chased me and some friends down the street after catching us ditching class. I made his working life hell during my tenure there and he made my social life hell. It was time for payback.

It's hard to say why I thought I was qualified to be the assistant principal. In fact, the position wasn't even open, but that didn't stop my psychotic thoughts from creating a totally plausible reality. It didn't help matters that the high school kids all thought this would be a great idea. I spoke with such confidence that they believed it was possible. I was still at the point in my manic adventure that I could make sense when I wanted to, and it was very easy for me to convince people that what I spoke was the truth. After all, I believed that everything I was saying was true, which made it a much simpler task. I imagine that this is the sort of feeling that aspiring cult-leaders must experience.

The lunch hour ended and they all went back to class. I assured them that I would be there at the end of the day to discuss matters further. I planned to spend the afternoon visiting old teachers in their classrooms, unannounced, uninvited and marvellously insane.

My first stop was to my field placement teacher. He had helped me to land my co-op position at the local newspaper the previous year. The placement had actually worked wonderfully. I had many front page articles and got to mingle with the many well-respected writers of the city. I guess I chose to visit this teacher because I knew he still sort of liked me and wouldn't kick me out.

We spent half an hour talking. Well, I did most of the talking. He listened, likely contemplating how the hell he was ever going to get me out of his office. I informed him that I had recorded a CD and that it was only a matter of days until I was world-famous. There were record labels contacting me from all over the world, so I just had to pick the one that would give me the most money. I also told him of my newfound genius IQ. I'm not sure where this delusion came from, because I certainly had never taken an IQ test, but it was the truth to me. I guess simply because my mind had never been running on so many cylinders at once, I just figured that this was what it must be like to be a genius. And since I believed my own mental creations, it made perfect sense.

It's hard to say if he believed what I was saying. I likely tried to remain as fluid as possible, as he was in a position of authority, but I will never truly know. Next on my journey was my creative writing teacher. We had gotten along excellently throughout high school. I was always the youngest person in her classes, as I would take English courses much above my current grade level. I knew she would welcome my presence with open arms, and she did.

She happened to be teaching the 'Writer's Craft' course at the moment which served my needs perfectly. She must have believed in some of my insanity as she asked me to address the class and discuss some of my successes in the writing world. Truthfully, I had some real, not imagined, successes that I could share, but I assume I spoke mostly of the ones that existed purely in my mind. I had the entire classroom in my hand. I spoke eloquently and passionately. Having access to the attention of thirty aspiring writers was the best, or worst, thing that could have happened to me in that frame of mind, and only served to feed my already enlarged ego to the point that new creations in my mind started becoming realities. By the time I was finished, I had an agent who was in talks with many publishing companies and my first novel was sure to be published within the year. The novel that I hadn't even written yet.

Everything was going great until the assistant principal came to the door of the class. Mr. Black was a very stern man. He would have done well in a position of authority in the military, which made him the perfect choice for assistant principal. He happened to be walking by the class and had heard the uproar coming from inside. And likely, my co-op teacher had informed him that I was in the building, wreaking havoc. He told me to come with him, so I did. He said he was calling the police and was going to have me charged with trespassing.

I didn't like that, so I ran. Down five flights of stairs at top speed and out the front door. There was no way I was getting charged with anything.

By the time I got off school property and caught my breath, I started to realize just how pissed off that had made me. All I was doing was trying to enlighten the lives of some aspiring writers. I guess he just didn't see it that way.

The school day was almost over, so I hung around the area. The smoking area wasn't on school property, so he could not have me charged with trespassing so long as I stayed there. Or so I thought.

The final bell rang and all the deviant smokers came out to join me once again. I was still fuming, and was quick to share my hatred for Mr. Black with the students. It wasn't hard to get them behind a fight against him, as they had often felt his wrath as well. As with most high schools, the smokers consisted of the burnouts, the musicians and every other type of kid that high school administrators did not particularly like.

I had a group of twenty or so students around me as I told them of being chased down the stairs and out the door by Mr. Black. They were mesmerized, and were hoping that the altercation was not over. I no longer went to school there, so I could get away with a lot more than they could.

Mr. Black noticed the huge group of kids circled around me and came outside. I started hurling insults at him at the top of my lungs. Within seconds, I had a group of teenagers joining me in yelling every derogatory term you could possibly think of at him. He tried to get me to leave, but there was certainly no way that was going to happen.

We yelled and argued back and forth for about five minutes. Little did I know that he had already called the police. Two cop cars pulled up and briefly talked to Mr. Black. Two officers stayed talking with him and the other two approached me. I was asked to come with them. When I asked them why, they explained that I was causing a disturbance.

Although I certainly did not agree with their position, I had more insight than to try and run away from the police. They didn't say they were charging me with anything so maybe I could talk my way out of it. And I did.

I got in the backseat of the cop car. They didn't handcuff me, as I wasn't arrested. This left me wondering what exactly they were going to do with me. My question was answered when we pulled up to the emergency room of the local hospital.

Now, I really had no idea what was going on. I wasn't sick. Why were they bringing me here? I walked in with the two officers. One of them talked to the girl at the desk and the other one sat beside me in the waiting room. I gave them my health card and sat as patiently as I possibly could. I kept asking the officer questions but they wouldn't give me the answers I was looking for. Apparently, I needed to talk to a doctor for some reason.

The other cop came and sat down on the other side of me. Being unfamiliar with the protocol then, I didn't realize that this was to keep me from running away.

Apparently when you are brought to the ER with two police officers, you get bumped up to the front of the line. A nurse came out and asked us to come with her; my cops and I obliged. She explained that the on-duty psychiatrist would be meeting with me. The police were instructed to stand outside the door and I was left inside, waiting. Psychiatrist? But why? None of this made any sense to me. If I had known then that this was the first--of many--attempts to have me committed, I likely wouldn't have been so calm.

I sat in the small office, fidgeting and reading every single thing on the walls. I studied anatomy from a graphic framed poster. The wait was likely only a few minutes but felt like days.

Finally, the doctor came in. He was an older man with white hair who actually seemed fairly nice. He explained that he was a psychiatrist and that, based on the conditions of my apprehension as well as what the police had noted upon meeting me, he'd been asked to conduct an evaluation into my state of mind. I thought this was fantastic. Finally, someone who was as smart as I was who would truly understand me. I was sick of being called crazy all the time. The doctor would surely have the ability to see that I was not only *not* insane, but that I was simply a misunderstood genius, a musical prophet, and an accomplished literary scholar.

The weird part is, I was actually able to convince him of all these things, and more. Sure, I was eccentric, but insane? Never.

I'm able to understand his error in medical judgement much easier now after working in the field of mental health. I have counselled people who have been found 'Not Criminally Responsible' and 'Unfit to Stand Trial' during my professional career. Some who had even killed multiple people while in the grips of psychosis, and I have yet to see a client who resembled the man I was in this doctor's office. Although most of what I said wasn't true, it could all possibly be true. I was smart enough to not talk about hallucinations or delusions of persecution, which I knew would immediately have me locked away. I still had enough common sense left that I was able to come off as perhaps a bit off my rocker, but nothing to really be worried about.

My claims of music stardom could be somewhat backed up by my schoolbag full of professional looking CD's, my writing exploits could be backed up with my stories of past accomplishments, and my high IQ could be back up by, well, just talking.

I tricked the psychiatrist, and was permitted to leave the hospital with no restrictions and no criminal charges.

After such an eventful afternoon and evening, I needed to relax. I went to Garvin's. And by relax, I certainly mean drinking copious amounts of liquor and snorting speed and ecstasy. I picked up a bottle of

Bacardi 151 on my way. It has something like 72 per cent alcohol content. This is a type of liquor that should not be sold to anyone, particularly someone who is already breaking the barriers of insanity. I knew a good night was about to commence.

Garvin and I started off with a few shots. Within what seemed like seconds, we were conducting experiments with the liquor. It was flammable, which was something very appealing to two people like us. We poured it down our arms and lit it on fire, a little more each time. There were a few other people there, as was the usual custom, and they simply could not believe what we were doing. It seemed fairly normal to me at the time though. I was glad to have a friend nearly as unbalanced as I was. It certainly helped me to feel that I wasn't insane, as the police and the parents and the principals were leading me to believe.

I spent the night at Garvin's and we got messed up beyond anyone's business. Another weird thing about mania is that alcohol seems to fuel it even more, instead of depressing the central nervous system, as it is supposed to. However, that could also be because of the massive amounts of stimulants that I was doing at the same time.

We ended up going to a bar later in the evening. We lasted about twenty minutes before we were forcefully ejected, and Garvin and I spent the rest of the night going from bar to bar, getting kicked out each and every time. It was like the world was against us. In reality, it was more like the world just couldn't handle us, and didn't even want to try. And I couldn't blame them.

After the bars had closed for the night, we brought some new friends back to Garvin's place. I was incredibly good at meeting people by that point. I could talk to anyone and could always find a way to get them to do what I wanted. In this case, it was getting a few good looking girls back to Garvin's place.

The party continued all night, and Garvin and I both got to have some drugged-up sex with some girls we happened to find that night. He lent me his spare room for the deed at hand. After the girl and I had finished, she quickly fell asleep, but sleep was not something that could come to me any longer. It had been many, many days since I had slept even for a few minutes and I wasn't going to start now.

I proceeded to go downstairs and clean every single inch of Garvin's house. I just had to keep busy. I felt as though my brain would explode if I ever stopped. It took me until morning, but by the time everyone woke up, the place was spotless. It might have been the first time his house had ever been so clean.

At around eight in the morning, I grabbed one of my CDs and headed off to the local radio station. Since, in my mind at least, I was already a famous musical genius, it felt natural to go to the radio station to do an interview and have them play some of my music, even though I wasn't invited, and they had no idea who I was. Somehow, in my deluded state, it had become true to me that I had actually been invited to the radio station and that they were going to help me get the fame that I so richly deserved.

At first I met with the secretary, who must have wondered what I was doing there in the first place. To this day, I'm not sure how, but I did end up in the DJ booth with the morning DJ. We talked music and he listened to my stuff during the commercial breaks. He seemed impressed, but it is worthy of noting that I didn't have the capability then to truly understand what other people were feeling. They felt what I thought they should feel. I had created, and was living in, my own reality, unencumbered by whatever 'real' reality was at play.

I didn't end up getting my music on the morning radio show, but I made a good connection at the station, or so I thought. It was much more likely that the DJ was simply nice to me because he wanted to get this crazy lunatic out of his booth. Regardless, I left the station a few hours later feeling as though I had truly accomplished something. When I related the story to my friends, it certainly sounded as if I did.

It's also important to note that you don't necessarily lie when you're manic. I guess the old adage goes 'it's not a lie if you believe it.' And that was the only truth I knew. No matter what *actually* happened, my mind created the perfect scenario of 'what should have happened' and that was my truth. So when I went around that day talking to people and telling them about my amazing experience on the morning radio show, I wasn't lying at all. In fact, it was the most honest thing I could have possibly said.

Since there isn't a whole lot going on in the morning in a small town in the middle of the week, I ended up at the mall. The mall was a paradise for me. People as far as the eye can see, all waiting to hear my fantastic stories of future world domination. I talked to strangers, I talked to people I knew. I just talked. And talked. And talked.

Somewhere along the line, I got the idea of trying to get some of the stores to play my music. I figured this to be an ingenious marketing opportunity, and strangely enough, it worked. After working my magic for about an hour, I had six stores in the mall all simultaneously playing my CD for their shopping public. I left my contact information with the store clerks for anyone who had heard the overhead music and wanted to buy the CD. I figured I would be selling hundreds of albums by the end of the day.

Although that didn't quite happen, it certainly didn't aid my failing sanity to be able to walk around the mall and hear my own music down every hall. It only served to increase the speed and intensity of my ego, and added a new flare to my psychosis. In my mind, I was famous. At least locally. The world was next.

When I left the mall, I headed back to home base at Garvin's. For perhaps the first time in history, no one was home, so I was left to my own devices. I had absolutely no money at all, but that didn't stop me from enjoying the finer things in life.

I headed over to a British pub and sat at the bar. I talked up the manager of the bar, who often had musical acts in the evening. Although I had no money in my pocket, and no possible way of getting any, I convinced him to start a tab for me. I had a club sandwich to start, and then began pounding down the beers.

I must have made a pretty convincing case to the bar manager, because I somehow convinced him to let me put on a concert in his bar that very evening. In my mind, it would be a glorious evening. My band would play through the night, win over the hearts of all the patrons and sell enough CD's to be able to pay off the bar tab. But there were a few small things that didn't come to mind as I made my pitch. Namely, the fact that I didn't even have a band. This would likely be a stumbling block for most people, but in my ravaged insanity, it literally never even occurred to me to be a problem.

I quickly made friends with the entire bar staff and within an hour had the run of the place. I was free to go behind the bar, into the kitchen, use the staff phone. Anything I wanted. And the beer and wings and whatever else just kept coming. If only they knew that I had about fifteen cents in my pocket.

I made some phone calls and told some friends of this amazing gig that I was planning and got as many of them to come down to the bar as possible. I had to get Garvin to bring a guitar, because, even though I was such a rock star, I currently did not have one in my possession.

Within a couple of hours, I had a good group of friends there who were all enjoying the free beer and the free eats on my tab. The bar had two levels, and the show was to happen upstairs. So my friends and I quickly took control of the upstairs portion and started getting ready for the big show. I'm sure one of them must have mentioned to me that I didn't have a band, or any gear, but I assume I quickly dismissed them.

The afternoon turned into evening and people started filing into the tavern. The more people, the more opportunity to talk, which equals more opportunity to plunge deeper and deeper into madness.

I played a few acoustic tunes for the small group of friends who had gathered early and it actually went quite well. I guess somewhere along the line I realized that I didn't have enough material to cover an entire night, so I quickly got on the phone and remedied the situation. I got a friend's band to bring their gear over and set up to take over the rest of the evening. And they brought their friends, and their friends brought their friends. It was a manic fantasy. The band was pretty tight and played a collection of their own tunes. Every few songs or so, I would force myself onto the stage and sing lead in a Weezer or Nirvana song. I even managed to sell a few CD's. A few, meaning less than ten, and certainly not nearly enough to cover the bar tab.

By the end of the night, the far-too-trusting bar owner brought me the bill. Since I had been buying rounds for everyone all night, it came to over $2,000.00. I had made about thirty dollars in CD sales. Reality started to rear its ugly head, so I did what any reasonable lunatic would do; I ran.

Since I had made it all too well-known who I was, it wasn't hard for him to track me down in the coming days, especially in a small city. My father ended up paying the tab on my behalf, something that I am extremely grateful for, although I certainly didn't show it at the time. I hadn't even seen him in weeks. My parents were the enemy. I just didn't realize that all they wanted to do was help me.

This night was my last memory of a somewhat happy insanity. Things got exponentially worse from there on in.

7

The Walls Start Closing In

After a stunt like that, it was becoming more and more difficult to convince people that I was of sound mind. Even my dearest friends started to have extreme doubts, and that contributed to the spiral of paranoia that would continue for months. I had had the world in my pocket, and now my pocket had been turned inside out and was attempting to devour me whole.

This was around the time that my two friends staged the intervention that I mentioned previously.

Their big thing during the intervention was that they wanted me to go to the emergency room, but I sincerely failed to realize exactly what this 'emergency' was. Since they were also only 18 years old, they had limited, if any, knowledge of insanity. They just knew something was terribly wrong and that I was not safe.

Things got ugly the night I went to the washroom upstairs and discovered Bryan on the phone talking to my parents. They had asked my friends if they could try to talk some sense into me, since no one else was having any luck. Viewing this as the ultimate betrayal, I lost it completely, again. All their credibility was now shot. They were working from the inside, for the man. I was onto them, and I would have nothing to do with their plan. My paranoia got worse, a lot worse. I left, and there was nothing they could do to stop me.

Although everyone experiences mental illness in their own unique way, my mania seems quite textbook, looking back on it now. I started off in the hypomanic stage where your mind works on a thousand cylinders and nothing had ever made more sense in my life. All my ideas are perfect; the solutions to all of life's problems found. This state can last, depending on the person, anywhere from a few days to even months and, in rare cases, years. But it can't last forever, which is what causes many afflicted people to seek stimulants such as cocaine, ecstasy and speed in order to keep the feeling alive. But after a while, your brain just can't take running on high twenty-four hours a day, without sleep. And then you enter the manic phase, which is characterized by unpredictable changes in mood, anger that can turn on a dime, paranoia, grandiose thinking and generally, a feeling that your mind is falling apart from the inside. Always wanting to get back to that hypomanic stage, which is impossible, you continue on your treacherous path and do as many drugs and drink as many drinks as you can, which in turn just makes it all worse. Or, at least that's what I did.

The next inevitable phase, once medication brings you back to reality, is depression. Not just your typical morning blues either. Wicked, painful, violent depression. Right now, for me, that stage was still many, many months away. The severity of the depression is usually correlated to the severity of the mania, I learned in my future professional experience. And my case was quite severe. I would later be told by psychiatrists that it was the most severe they had ever witnessed. When it was all said and done, I spent well over a year in a doomsday depression. It wasn't until a few years after that that I was able to start getting my life back on track.

The human mind is a beautifully wondrous thing. It tends to block out the painful memories as much as possible. That is why there aren't many memoirs written about manic or psychotic experiences. Typically, upon emerging from the madness, the sane mind cannot comprehend what just happened, and it is very rare to even have the energy to commit it to paper. This is compounded by the ensuing depression, which makes it hard to even get out of bed, let alone write a book. That also explains why this account comes eleven years after the fact. It wasn't until I had come to terms with myself, and made good on what I had done wrong, that I was able to sit down and think back to these times. Even after eleven years of reflection, there are some things that my mind still won't allow me to recall. Perhaps that's for the best. The things I do recall are terrifying enough on their own, so I'm not sure I would want to know the rest.

All this to say that I don't remember exactly how I ended up certified. Certified, meaning legally detained by the hospital because I was a 'danger to myself and others'. What I do know is that my father played a major part in making it happen. He petitioned a judge he knew to step in, because I kept on fooling the psychiatrists. The police picked me up and the hospital legally detained me by order of the courts. I was originally kept on an involuntary 72-hour psychiatric evaluation. Those seventy-two hours ended up turning into four months.

8

LOCKED UP AND LIVID

The next thing I remember is waking up in a hospital bed on the second floor of the general hospital. There were cold, iron bars on the windows and a security guard by my side. I had apparently been sleeping for quite some time, according to the security guard. They had injected me with a powerful anti-psychotic medication and given me enough sleeping pills to knock out a dinosaur. The only words I really remember the security guard saying were 'I'm really glad you got some sleep. You were pretty terrifying last night.'

There wasn't specifically a psychiatric unit at this hospital, but they did have a few highly secured rooms, just in case. It was very sterile, and very final. I checked the security of the bars on the window and soon realized that I would not be getting out through the window anytime soon. Therefore, there had to be another way.

I ate some hospital food that morning and kept on complaining to anyone who walked by that I wasn't allowed to go out for a cigarette. My security guard assured me that it wasn't up to him, and that I could ask the attending psychiatrist about it when he came to see me. I can assure you that that was the first thing on the agenda.

I don't remember the particulars of the psychiatrist that I met with that day, but I do recall that he explained briefly what was happening. I was being held for evaluation for 72 hours and the reason I was at the general hospital was because there currently wasn't any room available at the psychiatric hospital. I tried to get any information I could about my release date but he simply could not provide it to me. I imagine it was because by simply talking to me, he knew that I was in for a long haul and that immediate release was not even in the cards. I was still under the impression that I would be able to leave after the 72-hours. I thought they would just stamp me with my 'sane' card and let me go about my merry business. After all, that's what happened every time before.

Then he mentioned that if, at the end of the three days, they still felt I was a danger to myself and others, they could commit me indefinitely.

That just wasn't feasible for me. I didn't have time to spend my days locked away. I had missions to accomplish. I had a world to take over. They couldn't keep me. They just couldn't fucking keep me. Or so I thought.

The mountains of medication that they gave me certainly did calm me down physically. I wasn't running around constantly anymore and was able to sit for at least a few minutes at a time. I had procured a pencil and some paper, and I wrote feverishly for hours on end at the tiny desk in my room. I would love to have access to those papers today, as I'm sure they would be extremely interesting yet completely incomprehensible at the same time. Whereas the medication allowed me to finally be able to sit down, for the first time in weeks, it did nothing to quell the turmoil that was enveloping me from within.

For the seventy-two hours, probably more, I wasn't allowed to leave my room except to go to the washroom. And when I went to the washroom, they had to make sure there were no other patients there, and my security guard had to be right there with me. Watching me in the bathroom. Watching me. Every single thing I did. Twenty-four hours a day. *Watching me.*

I had gone from absolute freedom to being a bird locked in a cage. I thought it couldn't get much worse than this, but eventually, it did.

I brought the worst of it to myself. If I had behaved myself and acted like a good law-abiding lunatic, my hospital stay would have been much more pleasant. But acting normal isn't really an option when you are in the grips of psychotic rage and the entire world is conspiring against you.

I can't say that I remember a whole lot about those three days. The mind-erasing mania combined with the extremely powerful sedatives they had me on did a number on my memory. One thing that sticks in my mind is the looks on the faces of the other patients and their families when they walked past my room and saw the bars on my window and the security guard by my door. They were in the hospital for heart attacks, for surgeries, for physical therapy and other mundane reasons. They were certainly quite terrified of the kid down the hall with the long scraggly hair, the heavy beard and the look of lunacy in his eyes.

Since I didn't have a television, or anything really, in my room, all I did was write. I must have filled hundreds of pages with psychotic ramblings. I believed that they were brilliant words of wisdom. They dealt with the persecution I was going through at the hands of the medical world. How could they lock up someone, just for being brilliant? I was still nowhere even close to the point of admitting, or believing, that there was anything at all wrong with me. I was the sane one; people just couldn't handle me, and that wasn't my fault. I was a misunderstood genius. A prophet almost.

During those three days escape wasn't really an option. I was on the second floor, so I would have had to somehow subdue the security guard and run down the hallway, down the stairs, and past the main security station--which held numerous guards--and out the front door. Although I'm sure I contemplated it, I never attempted it. Even in the grips of madness, I guess I still had some concept of reality. I was fairly confident that I would be released after the 72 hours and would be free to continue my reign of eccentricity. The psychiatrist had something else in mind.

By the time the Form 1 72-hour psychiatric evaluation form had nearly expired, we had a meeting. There were several psychiatrists there, as well as a nurse and a medical doctor, and multiple security guards. It closely resembled a parole hearing and by the sheer volume of people on the other side of the table, I figured that good news did not await me.

The decision was that I still posed a grave danger to myself and others and that they were putting the paperwork through the courts to continue my detainment indefinitely. There was no longer an end-point. Whenever I was deemed better *by them*, I would be released. It could be days, it could be years. Figuring I had already lost everything I could have lost, I threw myself into a violent rage in the board room, screaming at the top of my lungs at the psychiatrists, hurling profanities at everyone in the room and attacking the security guards as they tried to detain me. They would pay, I assured them. Oh, they would pay.

I was brought out of the room forcefully by several security guards and strapped to my bed in a five-point restraint. Two leather cuffs around my wrists, two around my ankles and one around my waist. I made sure to not make it easy for them either. I tried to kick, punch and spit at anyone who came near. By the time it was all over and they had me locked to the bed, they all wished they had never met me. I'm sure my screams could be heard through the whole hospital floor for the next few hours. They injected me once again with an anti-psychotic and a sedative, and everyone but the main security guard left the room.

I was in a small, disinfectant smelling room, with prison decal bars on the window, strapped to the bed, screaming at the top of my lungs. Things had certainly gone from bad to worse.

I eventually fell asleep, due to the incredible amount of medication they had given me, and woke up less violent and angry. They took off the restraints in the morning and I was able to get up. I still couldn't leave my room, but at least I was no longer strapped to the bed. It was a small victory. Even when you are completely mad, you still have some concept of what is happening. However, it is extremely difficult to quell that voice in your head that tells you to act out when something doesn't go your way. But I was quickly realizing that these people meant business, and I was going to have to play by their rules. There is absolutely nothing in this world more dehumanizing than being strapped to a bed in a five-point restraint. Well, at least I thought so at the time. Had I been able to predict the future, I would know that there are far more awful ways that were used then to control the insane. They kept those secrets hiding away at the top of the hill on the outskirts of the city in the psychiatric hospital, just lying there, waiting for me.

Later that day, I was able to see the psychiatrist again. I recall telling myself to try to keep it together, because I now knew damn well what happens when you threaten the doctor. Thus, I remained as calm as possible and asked as many questions as I could.

'How long will I be here?' 'Why am I here?' 'When can I go for a smoke?' The smoking was a big issue for me. Not only because I was painfully addicted, but I knew that if I was just able to get outside, escape would be much easier.

The psychiatrist, perhaps thinking that I was gaining some lucidity, explained to me that if I was able to remain calm for the rest of the day, I could go out for a smoke that evening, with the guard, obviously. That worked perfectly for me. He also made the same deal regarding visitors. So long as I didn't cause the staff any more problems, I could have one visitor at a time.

He then went on to explain that I would not be kept at the hospital for much longer. They were working feverishly to secure me a bed at the psychiatric hospital. I didn't doubt his word, because I'm sure the nurses and the doctors and the patients on that floor wanted me out of there as soon as possible. But for now, I was here. My security guard and me.

I was given more privileges to walk around the floor as well. There was a TV room down the hall that I was allowed to sit in, as long as I remained calm. At the first glimpse of any disturbed behaviour, my guard had to the right to forcibly bring me back to my room.

It's truly remarkable that once you lose all freedom, how wonderful a tiny bit of it is. I certainly did not want to risk my time in the lounge by acting up again. Just being able to be out of my room, and not in restraints, was a wonderful feeling.

The guard and the nursing staff were all given the orders to reduce stimulation as much as possible for me. When you're in a psychotic manic state, anything can make you turn on a dime. Just being around other people would send me into a whirlwind. During my brief stints in the lounge, I could not focus for more than a second or two on the television, so I would try to talk to other patients, nurses, or anyone walking by. But this was against my care plan, so I was never able to stay there very long. They thought that putting me back in my room would calm me down, but it did nothing of the sort. When I was in my room, all I did was write. The writings were not organized in any way, but dealt mostly with the persecution I was feeling from all ends of the spectrum. I wrote pieces of poetry, tried to write my life story, wrote threatening letters to doctors and often went on written tirades against my father. By that time, I had either been told, or figured out, that he was the one who had put me in here. He became Enemy Number One. I hated him with every fibre of my being. How could my dad, who claimed to love me, lock me away like this? Although my dad wanted to visit, there was no chance in hell I was allowing that.

My mother, on the other hand, hadn't caused me any harm, so she was allowed to come and see me. This had to be only after a period of relative calmness and it was up to the charge nurse to decide if and when she was permitted to come. My poor mother did come and see me and we spent time in my room talking. Likely, I was the only one talking, as I didn't have the patience to listen to anyone else's voice but my own. Although I'm sure it must have been extremely difficult for her to see me in this situation, she remained strong, for me. I'm sure it killed her on the inside to hear me spew words of hatred against my father compounded by crazy theories of conspiracy. Her pleas of explanation that he was only looking out for my best interests fell on deaf ears, and I didn't realize it then, but I'm sure she had just as much to do with the decision as he did. That didn't matter. Black and white thinking was my speciality in that mindset, and my dad was on the outs. It would be many, many weeks before I permitted him to come and see me at the psych hospital.

My mom even went against everything she believed in and brought me cigarettes. She hated smoking, as would any good parent, but she realized that there were certainly more pressing issues on the table than my physical health. I would have loved to be a fly on the wall at the convenience store as my mother tried to figure out how to even order cigarettes.

I was, relatively speaking, calm, when my mom would visit, so I was allowed to go out for smokes with her and my guard. I wasn't about to put her through any more hard times, so I had no plans of trying to escape with her around. Being able to stand outside was a wonderful feeling. Having the cool winter air on my skin was a breath of kindness that I hadn't felt in days. And the thick, nicotine-laden smoke idling in my lungs brought back at least some sense of normalcy to my life.

After a few successful visits with my mother, I was permitted to have one friend at a time visit me. Of course, my 'real' friends wouldn't be coming anytime soon; they were terrified of me. The only people I could get to visit me were some of the shady characters that I had met during my insane romps through the city. I had become quite notorious and was something of a tourist attraction for the local stoners.

One girl, who was certainly nothing resembling a friend, came to visit me. She brought me a thermos filled with rum. How she got this past the nurse, I will never know but I was certainly thankful for it. However, I didn't realize just how difficult it would be to get drunk with a security guard within three feet of me at all times. I tried anyway.

Anyone who has ever drank rum knows that there is no mistaking the smell. It can envelop an entire room in seconds, and that's exactly what happened. The guard notified the nurse who came in and smelled the thermos. It was poured down the sink. I lost my mind, again.

Once again, I was screaming at the top of my lungs. And once again, the team of ogres came in and forcefully put me on the bed and applied the restraints. I would spend the rest of the night in restraints and that particular 'friend' was barred from visiting me again.

I'm not entirely sure how much of a setback that was, but presumably, I was kept in my room for at least a day for that violation. Having been restrained again only fuelled my intense hatred for everyone around me. It was time to get out of here.

I slowly gained back my privileges with good behaviour. First, I was allowed in the lounge for a few minutes at a time and eventually, I was again allowed out to the front lobby for smokes. I was allowed to bring two smokes with me, so my guard and I went down and I immediately lit one up. Coincidentally, a few more of my fake friends happened to be walking through the parking lot. The hospital was right on the route to downtown.

"Chris! Man, what the hell happened to you!?"

I explained that I was being held against my will and that the fuckers would pay. I was being persecuted against. Just you wait, I explained, I'll be out soon enough.

The security guard, respecting the rules of not allowing me much stimulation, told them to go on their way. But this tiny amount of stimulation secured my decision. My blood was now boiling, and I was revved up for action. I lit my second smoke.

The smoking area was about twenty feet by twenty feet. I slowly made my way to the very end of the area and made it appear as though I was lost in thought and deeply enjoying my smoke, while in my head, I was doing a countdown and taking inventory of my surroundings and planning my route. The security guard gave me some space as he likely didn't see me as an escape threat. I knew this, and used it to my advantage. As the countdown ended in my mind, I flew like an all-star sprinter across the parking lot. The emergency room and the security station were right by the front entrance and everyone could see what was happening. Within a few seconds, it wasn't only my security guard chasing me, but three others as well.

I ran like the wind. In fact, I was quite quick. I had run track in high school and was an avid basketball player earlier in my life. The sheer rush of insanity surely gave me an advantage, but what I didn't account for was the ice.

I got to the end of the parking lot and wiped out, falling right on my back. Before I had the chance to even realize what happened or to get up, they were on top of me. Never one to admit defeat, I fought back as hard as I could. Even being a small guy compared to the guards, I gave them a workout, but ultimately lost. They dragged me, kicking and screaming, back into the hospital. One of the guards at the guard station had radioed back to the unit I was being held on, so the charge nurse was aware of my latest stunt. They dragged me into the elevator. All four of them had at least one part of me secured. There was no escaping. I knew damn well what was going to happen next.

I was brought into the unit, still fighting as hard as I could, as more staff appeared to take me to my room. Once again, the straps came out and the needle went in. I had lost again. I would end up spending a very long time in restraints this time because I refused to calm down, and it seemed as though the medication they had been injecting me with was no longer working as wonderfully as it had at first. It was probably at least ten hours until I was slowly released from the restraints. Usually, they release the restraints after you wake up. But this time, I never fell asleep. I fought the medication as hard as I could and refused to fall asleep.

One limb at a time. They would untie one wrist, and see how I reacted. If I was a good boy, the next wrist would be freed. Then one leg, then the other leg and eventually the waist. I knew the process all too well.

Once I gained some semblance of freedom, I started the process again. I was determined to get back outside for a cigarette, but that wasn't going to be happening for a few days. During this time, I met with the psychiatrists again and reviewed what was happening with my pending transfer to the psych hospital. I asked a lot of questions about the psych. It was a scary thought. I remember that once he told me that there was a pool table there, I began to accept the idea much more easily. I had had enough of this place anyway, I was ready to continue to the next part of my journey. But, there still wasn't room at the inn, so I had at least another week here. I've often wondered what the final bill of my incarceration was for the taxpayers. Simply having a 24-hour security guard by my side would be costly enough.

After 'proving' myself for a while, I was once again able to have my mother come and visit. She made sure to not mention my escape attempt, as she did not want to aggravate me any further. I'm sure the charge nurse gave her a list of acceptable conversation topics before she entered the unit. The slightest thing could set me off, such as the mention of my father. His name was certainly not on the list of acceptable topics at this time. He had put me in hell. And for that, he could never be forgiven.

There was a specific security company that was contracted by the hospital to work on the grounds. I would estimate that they had about 15 employees who worked there, and I knew every single one of them.

Since they were the only people who had to be with me, they were my main source of entertainment. I soon knew most of their life stories. I was lucky enough to get a few nice ones who would actually talk to me, though there were a few who would just sit there, and ignore me. That just made me decidedly angrier. They were just security guards, however, and they weren't trained to deal with the mentally ill, so I couldn't hold it against them. But I did anyway.

A few of them were in school to become full-fledged cops, and those were the ones who took the assignment very seriously; they wouldn't give me any leniency at all. But since the only thing I could do at the time was observe my surroundings, I became quite aware of which ones I was able to fuck with, and which ones I couldn't.

One that I knew I couldn't fuck with was a future cop. Right at the beginning of his shift, he told me that if I even thought of attempting to run, he would tackle me to the ground. I believed him too. He had the build of a professional track star and I could see that I would be no match for him. Whenever he was on duty, I was on my best behaviour. But there was another security guard who had no aspirations of becoming a cop. We actually talked quite often. For him, this was just a job to pay the rent; he had no vested interest in it. For a security guard, he wasn't in optimal physical condition either. Although I hated to do it, since I had grown to like him, I knew that he was going to be the key to my freedom. If he had known what I was thinking, he likely wouldn't have been so nice to me.

As the routine goes, I was slowly given more and more privileges. I was once again allowed out for smokes, but the guards were told to remain as close to me as possible. They just couldn't risk me trying to escape again. It didn't look good on the hospital and it certainly didn't look good on the security company. Due to these heavier restrictions on my freedom, I knew I had to be creative with my next attempt. I couldn't do this alone.

The guard that I knew I could bend started his shift at 3PM one day. I knew I would have the next eight hours to plan and execute my strategy. I had gained access to a phone in my room. Typically, the guards would give me some space on the phone and wouldn't really listen in. I had called another one of my stoner friends and enlisted her help. I told her to borrow some clothes from her brother and bring them for her visit.

The plan was this: she would come visit and we would go out for a smoke together, with the guard. She would have the clothes in her backpack that I could put on afterwards, when we met up at a mutually agreed upon location. I knew police reports always consisted of clothing, so if I was able to change clothes, it would make getting out of the area much easier. Once we were outside, she would start flirting with the guard to get his attention away from me. Once he was sufficiently distracted, I would run. I had another stoner friend living only a few blocks from the hospital and she made sure that he was home and ready to take me in. Once I got there, she would meet me there with the clothes and I would be home free. I didn't need to plan farther than that. The big issue was getting off the property. Once I was in my friend's home, there was no way they would find me. It seemed like a good plan, but as in all escape attempts, there is always something that you don't take into account.

She arrived in the early evening and we went out for a smoke. She had the backpack on and through eye contact only, assured me that the plan was a go. Thankfully, there weren't many other people outside in the smoking section right then. I had a few things in my favour; first, I knew that this particular guard wasn't prepared to chase me, and even if he did, wouldn't be able to catch me. Also, he had no vested interest in this job, so likely didn't really care all that much in the first place. And also, I knew from our conversations, that he was single and lonely and thus, would respond quite well to a pretty girl showing him some interest.

This 'pretty girl' was another one that I had met during my times on the outside. We had slept together once, simply because she wanted to 'know what it's like to fuck a crazy person.'

Although she wasn't a stand-up person, she was the perfect addition to my team, and did her job wonderfully. She started working on the guard almost right away, in my room. That way, it made it less obvious that something was up when she began hitting on him outside. She was smart, in a devious sort of way. I guess, much like me.

We got outside and she and I each lit a smoke. I was allowed to bring two, so I made sure to fully enjoy the first one before attempting anything. Also, I had to give her time to work her magic. Slowly, I began to distance myself from them. The guard likely thought that this was because I was nice enough to give them some privacy, since she was obviously so enthralled with him. I actually felt bad in the days after about deceiving this guard, since he had been nothing but nice to me, but I was a professional manipulator and I used his kindness against him.

My planned route was quite different from the last attempt. Since I needed to eventually get to my friend's house, I had to aim for that general direction. I wasn't dumb enough to run straight for it. When they started looking for me, they would go in the direction that I ran. So although his apartment was basically a few blocks away, straight ahead from the front door of the hospital, my plan was to run to the left. Then eventually, I would circle around the back streets and end up at his house. In theory, the cops would be looking on the left side of the hospital, while I was in front of it, a few blocks down.

I lit my second smoke and enjoyed it thoroughly. I recall thinking that the next smoke I have would be in the freedom of my friend's living room. Soon, I would be able to get back to business. The business, of course, of becoming famous, or at least, more famous than I already thought I was.

When the time was right, I signalled to my friend and two seconds later, ran like the wind down a cleared path on the side of the hospital. It had been laced with salt and sand to keep the ice at bay, so I was free to run as fast as humanly possible. In a matter of seconds, I was off the property. It was only then that I looked back to see if the guard had given chase. I was very pleased to see that he had not. Everything was going according to plan.

It was around then that I started to realize a few things that I had neglected to take into consideration. Namely, I couldn't walk down the street, because I would be picked up in seconds. Therefore, I had to run through backyards, which would have been fine in the summer, but it was the dead of winter and there were several feet of snow on the ground. But I had to think on my feet and jumped through the snow bank into the first backyard.

I went about a block down, traveling through backyards, when I decided to stop. Most people's lights were off in their homes, so I wasn't worried about being seen. And in the winter, most people aren't spending time looking into their backyards, especially at night. I couldn't just stay forever in the backyards; I had to get to my friend's house.

I hunched behind a snow bank, hidden from the street, and waited and watched. I was a few blocks away but I could still see the hospital quite clearly. There were always two or three police cars parked in the front of the hospital and I noticed that they were now gone. I was correct to assume that they were looking for me.

After such a quick sprint in difficult terrain, I had to catch my breath. I saw a cop car coming down the street, his spotlight on. I lay down behind the snow bank. Shit was not going according to plan. He was shining the light into yards all down the street. I had to get inside. I would only be safe inside someone's home.

I made the decision to try to lie my way into someone's house so I could call for a cab. I didn't have any money for a cab, but I simply would have gotten him to drop me off some place far away, and then jumped out on the fare. When you're evading the police, you aren't really too concerned with ripping off cabbies.

I waited patiently in the snow bank until I no longer saw any cop cars. They were likely checking out the other streets. It was a very suburban neighbourhood with many criss-crossing streets. I could be anywhere.

When the coast was clear, I ran straight across the road to a house that had lights on. I knocked on the door and waited, quietly freaking out and worried that the cops would spot me, until the man inside opened the door.

I explained in a rushed panic that I was being chased by a bunch of drug addicts who were trying to beat me up and Bob me. Please, if you could just let me stand inside the door and call a cab, I would be ever so grateful.

I was talking a mile a minute, but that seemed to go along with my story. If I actually was being chased, I likely would have been in a similar frantic state.

He handed me the phone and I called the cab. I waited by the door, opening the blinds every few seconds just hoping that the cab would show up. I knew that when the cab showed up I would be home free, but until then, everything was up in the air.

I'm still not sure entirely how the next event happened. Perhaps the man who opened the door put two and two together and realized that I wasn't running away from Robbers, but that I was running away from the police, and went in the other room to phone them. Or perhaps the police were told by a neighbour that I was there. It's tough to say, but it didn't matter why in the end. They knew where I was.

The spotlights shone through the front door of the house and the man yelled at me 'There's your fucking cab. Get the fuck out of my house!'

There were three cop cars parked haphazardly across the street and in his driveway. I knew the jig was up. I opened the door and stepped out onto the porch. One cop was standing in the driveway and had his gun pointed at me. I had an eerie smile on my face, somewhat proud of all the attention that I had brought upon myself.

"Put your hands on your head and don't move or I will shoot you!" he yelled. I quickly abided. There were six cops in total; quite the showing. The cop with his gun drawn took charge and, along with two other officers, rushed over and grabbed my hands from above my head. Within a second, they had my hands behind my back and the cuffs on. Tight. Extremely tight. I ended up with punctures on my wrists.

The lead cop yelled at one of the other cops to check inside the house and make sure the occupants were all okay. I told him that I never had any intention of hurting anyone. I was actually offended that he felt the need to see if they were ok. I wasn't a criminal. Why were they treating me as one? He told me to shut the fuck up, and they tossed me in the back of the cruiser.

I had no issue with fighting off security guards, but I knew better than to try to fight cops. Particularly pissed off cops. They left me in the back of the cruiser for about ten minutes. They made sure that everyone in the house was ok, which I'm sure they were, albeit a little shook up. It isn't every day that something like that happens in the suburbs.

Once they had the situation contained, two cops got in the car and drove me back to the hospital. Another cop car followed and one stayed on the scene. It was only a few seconds' drive back to the hospital. I hadn't really gotten that far, but sure had caused a lot of pandemonium in what couldn't have been more than half an hour since I ran.

They pulled up to the front door. Four cops opened the door of the cruiser and dragged me out. They weren't taking any chances with me. With wrists bound behind my back, they dragged me into the front lobby. It actually felt pretty cool. I had done something so bad to warrant four officers bringing me in. The people in the halls couldn't contain their intrigue. I'm sure they wondered why I wasn't being taken to the police station. That's the beauty of being declared insane by a psychiatrist. No matter what you do after that diagnosis, they can't put you in jail.

Although I wasn't even fighting back, the cops were still extremely forceful as they brought me back to the ward. In my mind I was already preparing the details of my lawsuit. A few nurses and orderlies met us when we got onto the ward and they quickly brought me to my room. The cops held down my limbs as the nurses attached the restraints. I wasn't physically fighting, but I also wasn't being compliant. I was yelling about how I was going to sue them all and that there was no way they were going to get away with this. The restraints were put in place much tighter than any previous time. It doesn't matter, though. Once they are on you, there is no way of getting out. Putting them on tighter was just their way of showing me how pissed off they were at all this extra work they had to do. I can only imagine the paper work involved when a patient has to be brought back to the hospital by four cops.

When I was secured to the bed, the cops and nurses all made me painfully aware that I had fucked up, big time. I wasn't getting out again. That was the final straw. And true to their word, that was the last time I felt natural air on my skin for over three months.

9

SOLITARY INSANITY

I stayed in the restraints all through the night. They drugged the hell out of me, so I was able to get a bit of sleep at least. By the time morning came, my world started to change dramatically.

The next three months would become the most life altering, and mind altering that I would ever experience, and certainly nothing that I would wish upon my worst enemy.

When the business day started, the psychiatrist and nurse came into my room, ignoring my pleas to let me out of the restraints. They had bigger things in mind. It seemed my latest 'adventure' had magically made a bed appear at the psych hospital. I was to be transferred within the hour. Until then, I was staying in the restraints. They weren't taking any more chances with me.

A bit later on, a nurse came into my room and packed my belongings for me. She wouldn't even acknowledge me, even though I did all I could to get her attention. Everyone on that floor was at their wits end. This was certainly not in their job description. They weren't use to housing the insane, especially the violent and prone to escape insane. They couldn't wait to get me out of there.

All of my worldly possessions were packed into a few bags, then two cops showed up at my door. The nurse explained to me once again that I was being transferred to the psych hospital and that the cops would be taking me there. The nurse undid the restraints, and the cops put me into handcuffs. I was led through some back stairs to the back of the hospital, away from public view, to the back of a waiting cruiser. I had calmed down by then, so they weren't forceful, but weren't overly polite by any means.

In the cramped back seat of the cruiser I wondered what could possibly be awaiting me. By the sheer intensity of what had happened in the past twelve hours, I knew it couldn't be good. We pulled away from the hospital property and headed to the outskirts of town. I knew nothing of this psych hospital besides the urban legends about town. It sounded like an awful place, and I tried to convince myself that that couldn't be the case. Unfortunately, I was wrong. It did indeed live up to the legend.

It was about a ten minute drive out of the city. I had never even been near it, and didn't know where it was located. When I saw it through the cop car door approaching on the right side, there was no mistaking it. Surrounded by miles and miles of forest, it was a ridiculously large, sprawled out building, kept far, far removed from society.

This hospital was built in the early 1900's and was an exact replica of what comes to mind when you think of the old time psych hospitals in horror films. It could have easily been the set of *One Flew Over the Cuckoo's Nest*. Thankfully, at the time of this writing, it is no longer in use. It has been relocated to the city into a state of the art hospital that serves both medical needs as well as psychiatric. There has been a move across North America in the past decades to bring mental health treatment back into the public eye and to create more civil surroundings for the patients. That didn't matter then. I was going here now, to hell on Earth.

The cruiser pulled off the highway onto the swerving roads that served the hospital. I was amazed by its sheer enormity. I later learned that much of it had been condemned and was no longer even in use. After about a fifteen minute drive, we ended up in the back of the hospital next to an ominous garage door that was used to bring patients inside.

The cops let me out and led me through the garage door which quickly closed behind us. We went down a confusing mess of hallways. The paint was all chipped and falling off, the walls were a mishmash of yellow, pink and green, all fading after decades of being neglected. We went to an office where one of the cops got someone who worked there to meet us. With the cuffs still on, I followed them quietly through the halls. The new person, whom they did not even bother introducing me to, used a special swipe card to open a large steel door. The door slammed behind us and I looked back at it. You could just tell by looking at it that it was the type of door that no one who wasn't supposed to get through had ever gotten through. We entered a small exam room and the cops removed my cuffs.

I sat down. The cops filled out some paperwork and were soon gone. It was just me and this mysterious person, who apparently now had control over my entire life. I had to strip down completely, and another unknown person entered the room. They checked me out physically and performed a cavity search. It was perhaps the most demeaning moment of my entire life. There was no mistaking that my life had come to an abrupt halt.

They asked me a million questions as they filled out a million forms. They gave me some hospital gowns to put on. I sat in the chair, quiet and defeated. There was no point in fighting anymore. Well, at least not yet.

After what seemed like hours, they let me out of the tiny room and one of the mysterious men showed me around the unit. Everything about it screamed insanity. There were people screaming at the tops of their lungs to no one in particular. People were wandering about, looking extremely lost. It was everyone for themselves. The staff didn't even seem to acknowledge that the patients were there. The walls were faded and falling apart. The paint hadn't been redone in what seemed like decades. It reeked like urine and puke.

The nurses' station was right across from the room they had me in. It was located right at the entrance of the unit, and was surrounded by glass, presumably, bullet-proof. Then there was a long hallway with tiny rooms along the sides filled with examination beds, medical books and files. On both sides of the hallway, it opened up into two large dorm areas. The women were on the right side dorm and the men were on the left. It was expressly explained that the men stayed on their side and the women stayed on theirs. If a man was found in the woman's dorm, there would be a price to pay. Each dorm had about fifteen beds in it, and they were spaced only a few feet apart. I was shown to my bed, right next to all the other crazy people.

Further down the hall, there was a smoking room. This was the first good news I had received in days. We were allowed to smoke pretty much anytime, except between 11 PM and 7 AM. At the very end of the hall, there was what was called the day room. It had a TV, some disgusting ratty old furniture, and some board games. Off to the left was a pool table. I remembered thinking once before I arrived that 'hey, it has a pool table, so it can't be that bad.' Playing pool was the furthest thing from my mind.

The one thing the mysterious man didn't show me during the tour was 'The Bubble Room.' I would soon enough become extremely familiar with it, so a tour wasn't necessary. I guess they figure only a small percentage of the patients will ever have to go in The Bubble Room, so there is no need to terrify everyone with it right away.

At the end of the tour, I didn't know what to do with myself. What could you do? I asked one of the nurses for the cigarettes from my bag and found a spot in the disgusting smoking room.

Entering the smoking room was like entering death row. It reeked of stale cigarettes and you could barely even see across the room through the clouds of smoke. Patients sat, staring and chain-smoking. Some spoke to themselves, a few spoke to each other. I knew after one quick glance that not one of them could have passed for sane. It was terrifying. I wasn't one of *these* people. Why did they have me here? Something horrible had happened. This couldn't be happening. It just couldn't be.

Having no other choice, I settled onto the ward as much as was humanly possible. I had a little night stand beside my bed in the dorm and I set up camp there with my pads of paper and pencils and tried to make sense of what was happening around me through my writing. There was no making sense of it. Even if I had my sanity, I couldn't make sense of this awful place.

I eventually met my psychiatrist, Dr. Dougson, who would be responsible for my care throughout my stay there. She was a middle-aged lady who was reasonably nice, and I only got to see her once a day for a few minutes. The rest of the time I was left under the 'care' of the nurses and orderlies who hated working there as much as the patients hated being there.

Though there were exceptions to the rule, they were generally mean-spirited people who did not give a rat's ass about the comfort level of the patients, whom they treated as criminals instead of as people with an illness who needed to be cared for. It was certainly a far cry from an environment conducive to getting better.

Dr. Dougson explained that she would be trying some new medications on me. She had been briefed on my history and had read all that she could about me. We talked, but most of what I said didn't make much sense, I'm sure. My entire life was in her hands, and I have to say that, in retrospect, she did the best she could, given the circumstances.

I'm sure I was told then what the medications were; I have never been able to recall them since. I certainly wish I could though, for I have often wondered about their side-effects, and also what was listed as their beneficial effects. I was already one of the craziest people in the city, and I was about to get a fuck of a lot crazier. But without knowing the names of the medications, it's hard to explain exactly why. My mother often thought that the medications were responsible for making me worse, which is entirely possible. But it was likely a combination of medications that didn't agree with me, coupled with being locked in this reprehensible place that contributed to my further downfall from reality.

10

The Bubble Room

The first few days were relatively event-free. I was too terrified of my surroundings to act out and for the most part, I kept to myself. I didn't want to associate with the other patients and had nothing to say to the nursing staff. I did my writing and I chain-smoked. I absolutely despised the dormitory set-up for the sleeping arrangements.

People in the throes of insanity don't usually sleep well. Their sleep is fragmented by weird sounds, screams, and bizarre movements. It was nearly impossible to get any rest, always feeling that you need to keep one eye open.

There was one particular patient who really got on my nerves. His name was Clint and he was about my age. I guess he thought that since we were close in age, we should be best friends. I still to this day, even with my formal psychiatric training, have no idea what his diagnosis would have been. All I knew was that he was the most annoying person I had ever met in my entire life. He refused to leave me alone and followed me wherever I went.

One day I couldn't take it anymore, and I attacked him. I put my hands around his neck and tried to strangle him as hard as I could.

The staff was always on guard for situations like this and they quickly had me in their grips. Five large orderlies appeared, seemingly out of nowhere, and took me away. They informed me that I was going to the Bubble Room and brought me there with force. I couldn't believe that I was the one being punished for him being such an annoying fool.

The name of the room came from the fact that there is a gigantic shatterproof bubble on the outside of the room that allows staff to stick their heads inside so that they can see the entire room. It is the equivalent of a padded room that you often hear about in books and movies. The only difference being that it wasn't padded at all. It was a cold, hard, barren room with nothing inside but a small mat on the floor. No windows, no way out. Solitary confinement. This was soon to become my new home. During the first two months there, I likely spent more time in the Bubble Room than anywhere else on the ward.

Anyone who acted out in any way got sent here. They said it wasn't meant as a punishment, but as a place to calm down. However, I fail to see how putting a patient in solitary confinement in a dark, empty room has any therapeutic benefit whatsoever. It was the Bubble Room that I believe contributed to my sharp fall from just plain madness, to a whole new degree of psychosis that couldn't be paralleled.

I have no idea how long I spent in the Bubble Room the first time. There is no way of keeping time, as there is no natural light, no clocks, no way at all to keep any sort of sense of time. What I do know, is that when they eventually let me out, I was far more aggravated and psychotic than when I went in.

Also, you never get sent to the Bubble Room without a healthy dose of a powerful sedative, or an anti-psychotic. Since there was no bed in the Bubble Room, just a mat on the floor, the orderlies had to pin me down to the ground so that the nurse could give me the injection. And once the needle was in, everyone left and the door slammed shut. This was supposed to make you better.

Having nothing to pass the time, I counted. I walked in a square around the room counting my steps out loud. You weren't allowed having paper or a pen or a book, or anything at all to occupy your mind. Counting was all I had.

It took four steps on each side to circle the room. So I walked in the square, counting, counting, counting. One, two, three, four, five, six, seven, eight, nine, ten, eleven, twelve, thirteen, fourteen, fifteen, sixteen.

Repeat.

Repeat.

Repeat.

They eventually let me out, but the person they sent in there and the person that came out were no longer one and the same.

My paranoia had only been getting worse in the past few days. And now, in this new, terrifying scenario, paranoia was all I had left. I believed that the staff were all against me, and I had plenty of evidence to support that. Had they not been against me, they wouldn't have put me in that awful place. I was planning my retaliation.

When I got out of the Bubble Room I found out who my nurse of the day was. It was a heavy-set guy in his mid-thirties named Rob. I tracked him down on the unit and tried to ask him a few questions about my new home, and their use of the Bubble Room. However, I was still extremely psychotic and prone to quick bursts of anger, and as it turns out, Bob was the last person I should have been talking to. He was a pig-headed, macho brute, certainly not someone who should have been working in the field of playing with minds. If he decided to answer me at all, it would be with quick, one word answers. He viewed his job as solely a medication provider and hated when the patients actually tried to interact with him. He should have been nicer to me. He really should have been.

After a few hours of Bob ignoring my pleas for someone to please explain to me what was going on, I took the situation into my own hands. He was walking down the main hallway with his back to me. I yelled out something to him to try to get his attention. Upon being ignored again, I ran at him and jumped on his back, wrapping my forearm around his neck as hard as I could. I was trying to strangle him. In other outbursts, it was debateable whether or not I had a plan. This time, the plan was simple: I wanted him dead.

He had at least one hundred pounds on me, but my sheer anger and psychosis initially gave me the upper-hand. He fought back as hard as he could but I stayed hanging on, firmly gripped around his neck. He let out a bellowing scream and the Code White alarm went off. The nurses' station emptied and everyone came running to his rescue. I was grabbed by two orderlies and dragged onto the floor. Bob was swearing at me at the top of his lungs. I swore back.

More orderlies came and I was dragged back into the Bubble Room. I wasn't going down without a fight this time. I got a few good body shots and a couple of hits to the faces of the gigantic orderlies, which only served to piss them off even more and caused them to secure a tighter grip. A nurse held the door to the Bubble Room open and they threw me in. The door closed. I wondered why there was no needle. It was on its way. I guess they needed a break from me and wanted to make sure Bob was OK before continuing.

Maybe ten minutes later, a nurse popped her head in the bubble. "Chris, your doctor has ordered another injection. Are you OK with us coming in there and giving it to you?"

"Bring it on," I said, revved up and ready to fight.

The door swung open and eight people entered the Bubble Room; two nurses and six orderlies. I hid with my back against the wall, trying to protect myself at first. When they got too close, I started throwing fists. They were more prepared this time, however, having had the chance to cool off. They tried to grab my limbs all the while yelling at me 'just fucking calm down, stop fighting us!'

I was wearing only slippers on my feet and one of the orderlies, who I guess was quite sick of dealing with me, decided to use a little trick he must have learned in his years on the job to subdue patients. He lifted up his booted foot and stomped on my toe as hard as he could. I fell to the ground screaming in pain. They were easily able to grab my limbs and administer the shot. Almost before it began, it was over. They all filed out of the room as quickly as they could.

I was left lying on the ground, screaming out in pain. It felt as though my toe was broken. I held it and screamed at the top of my lungs. Those mother fuckers! Those fucking mother fuckers!

The screaming didn't stop. I was screaming about how I was going to sue them. I was screaming for them to let me out. I was screaming just for the sake of screaming. There was nothing left to do.

My toe was in agonizing pain. To this day, I still have a scar there to remind me of the brutality that I endured at the hands of the supposed helpers. Now, my paranoid delusions were certainly becoming true. They *were* against me. And since they were the only ones here, that meant *everyone* was against me.

I didn't calm down for hours. I later found out that I kept the other patients awake that night with my screams. I didn't even realize it was night time. They brought me another injection. I still fought back, but I was basically disabled by the orderly crushing my foot, so I didn't give them quite the same run for their money.

At one point, I managed to calm down and survey the situation. It was extremely hard to collect one's thoughts while in this shoebox hell, but the thoughts that I was able to corral indicated to me that my life was now over. I had nothing else to live for and there was nothing else to lose. I started banging my head as hard as I could against the cold, hard walls. I tried different approaches too. I would sit in front of the wall and bang it repeatedly. Then I would take a run at it and try to cause as much damage as I possibly could. It was as though I couldn't feel pain anymore. I knew that this likely wouldn't kill me, but it was the only thing that made sense at the time. Pain was the only thing that was real anymore.

Besides a few nurses sticking their heads in the bubble and telling me to stop, they didn't care a whole lot what I did to myself in there. So I banged my head, again, again and again.

I must have been in there for over 24 hours that time. I knew the next day had come because my psychiatrist was back on the floor. I never really had anything against her, so I was happy to see her poke her head into the bubble.

"Chris. Would you like to talk? I'm going to come in, with a few orderlies, OK?"

The orderlies were there purely for her protection, but I never had any intention of harming her. It was them who needed protection from me. It was one of their own who had maimed me, and for that, they would pay.

The doctor and I talked. I fumed about the assault on my foot. She assured me that she would look into it and also advised me that I had the right to speak to the Rights Advisor. This was a lawyer for the floor who dealt with clients' complaints, quite possibly the worst job on Earth, as people in the grips of psychosis are constantly trying to file frivolous lawsuits. However, it was my right to speak with him, and I was going to take full advantage of that.

Dr. Dougson explained to me what was going to happen next. "We're going to give you a needle. It what's called a long-lasting injection. Basically, it will make you feel like you just smoked a bunch of pot for the next 24 hours. If you're able to remain calm for the next hour, we'll let you out of the Bubble Room."

The idea of being high on pot for 24 hours seemed pretty appealing, so I did not have any objections. I was aware that there was no point in objecting anyway, because what they say, goes.

So for the first time, I let them inject me without fighting back at all. It was her calming presence that made all the difference. And, I wanted to get the hell out of there as soon as possible.

I got the injection and just laid on the mat. Within a matter of minutes, it took me over. I recall thinking that she must never have smoked pot before, because this sensation was about 50-times more potent than any pot I had ever smoked. I focused on enjoying the high, and I calmed right down. Within the hour, I was back on the outside. Which, ironically, is still on the inside.

Wanting nothing at all to do with the nursing staff anymore, I started talking to the other patients. I went immediately to the smoking room. It was there that I was informed by the patients that I had kept most of them up all night with my screams. I didn't really care though.

A few of them were really pissed off at me. I really couldn't give a flying fuck what they thought. I was no longer scared of them - I was crazier than they were. If they even thought of messing with me, I would run at them with everything I had. I knew what happened if I was violent, and I could handle it. The Bubble Room had nothing on me anymore. It was no longer a threat. Whenever I felt an urge, I acted on it. If that urge was violent, it wasn't my problem.

I don't remember the first time that J.T. and I spoke, however, he does. He went on to become one of my best friends and is still someone that I keep in close contact with today. In fact, as I write this, I am glad to have had him around, as he has served as my memory guide to many of the things I have either blocked away, or was just too drugged up to remember.

J.T. was then, and is today, one of the most fascinating people I have ever met. In my psychosis, I was drawn to him. We were quite similar. However, the ways in which we'd each ended up in this place were far removed from one another. We were on the opposite ends of the spectrum. J.T. was extremely depressed and I was extremely manic. Together, we were the 'Bipolar Bears.'

He was in the midst of a drunken crime spree when he was apprehended by the police. When he pleaded for them to shoot him in the head instead of taking him into custody, he ended up here. His world was also over. He wanted to die.

We sat at a table in the day room and he told me, like many others had, that I had kept him up all night. I apologized for this, but he wasn't seeking an apology. He had been admitted when I was in the Bubble Room. He also didn't know anyone else there, and he also, did not want to be there.

He tells me I informed him that I had a personal helicopter that was going to come and get me out of this place. All I had to do was place one phone call, and the helicopter would be on the roof. I offered him a ride to wherever in in the world he wanted. He agreed to tag along, just playing along with my psychosis. After all, he was depressed, but still had a fairly good concept of reality. I hadn't known what reality was for many months now and my delusions were getting more and more intense.

We spoke for hours. I told him about the assault on my toe and showed him my wounds. I told him of my vile hatred for Rob. He shared the same hatred, having had only one encounter with him. When you're depressed, it's hard to put together a sentence sometimes. He later told me that he was thankful for our conversations because my psychosis would distract him from his own issues. I was just so fucking out of it. It was entertaining for him. We soon became inseparable. It was him and I versus the hospital. And versus the world.

That night would be the last that I would spend in the dorm for quite some time, though I can't recall exactly why. But I can make an educated guess that I once again attacked another annoying patient or perhaps another staff member. I ended up in the Bubble Room again, drugged out of my mind.

In the morning, Dr. Dougson came to visit me in the Bubble Room. She explained that I would be getting my own room. I wondered how this was possible, since there were no single rooms on the unit. She told me that they were transforming one of the file rooms into my own personal room. Currently, they were removing all the boxes of files and other nursing gear and would be putting a bed and a night table in there. Finally, my uncontrollable violence was paying off.

The room was directly across from the nurses' station. They could no longer trust me alone in the unit. They needed to have eyes on me at all times. She also explained that I would be on Constant Observation when I emerged from the Bubble Room. C.O. means that you are a major threat to yourself and others on the unit and that there will be a designated staff person, either a nurse or an orderly, assigned to be with you 24 hours a day, much like what I had experienced with my security guards. I didn't mind. I had my own room and my own personal assigned friend.

I eventually was let out of the Bubble Room and was shown to my new room, and my constant observer. I had so many of them during my stay there that I don't have many specific memories of who they were. One thing I do know is that it was never Rob. I made a plea with the Rights Advisor to have him removed from my care plan. He would no longer be assigned as my nurse and he wasn't even allowed to talk to me. As far as my lawsuit about the toe, it didn't get very far. It was a psychotic man's word against the medical staff's, and they'd made no mention of stomping on my toe in their notes. I bitterly accepted the defeat.

The room was all right. In fact, it was better than all right. Anything was better than the awful dorm set-up. They had hoped that separating me as much as possible from the other patients would serve to calm me down. And for a while, it did. My mother brought in a bunch of books and magazines for me and I had enough pencils and pieces of paper to last me a year. For the most part, I was confined to my room while on Constant Observation, at least at first. They wanted to reduce stimulation as much as possible, so I ate my meals in there and counted the hours down in there. The orderly had a chair at my door. Besides other patients and nurses walking down the halls, he was the only one I could talk to. Sometimes J.T. would stop by my doorway and visit, but the nurses always shooed him away. Too. Much. Stimulation. Makes. Chris. Go. Crazy.

I guess their little plan worked. It was hard to be violent having someone within three feet of you at all times. Without any 'stimulation' it was hard to find a reason to get pissed off. And my constant observer also served as my secretary. Whenever I needed something mentioned to the doctor or nursing staff, they would take care of it. On a ward that had no single units, I had a single unit. I was officially the craziest person in the crazy house. That sort of thing commanded respect among the other patients as well. I was all but assured that no one would risk trying anything with me from this point on.

11

'I'm Not Here; You're Crazy'

I was on constant observation for about a week, and I guess I must have calmed down, because it was eventually lifted. I was now again free to roam around on the highly secured unit. And now I had a friend, a partner in crime. If J.T. hadn't been there, I think my stay would have been much, much worse.

He was an extremely talented artist and was always feverishly working on some sort of drawing. Since I had no artistic talent, at least in drawing form, we would often combine forces with my ideas, and his brush strokes. There was one particular piece that I held onto for many years after. I had planned on getting it tattooed to my chest. Although it was a beautiful drawing, I am now glad that I didn't get it done, as it would have been a very morbid thing to have to explain to potential romantic partners upon removing my shirt.

It was a tree. One half of the tree was bursting with life, with beautiful foliage and healthy branches. On one of the branches, a child's swing was held and a kid swung happily. The other half of the tree was dead, and broken. No more leaves, and the branches were rotting and falling apart. On one of the branches, there was a man, hanging from a noose. The child was unaware of the swinging torso just feet behind him.

J.T. also drew a bunch of art that I planned on using in future CD booklets. I was writing music under the pseudonym Caparosa, the name I'd used on the *Soap and Towels* demo CD that I recorded on the outside. It was a name and a concept that had come to me during the grips of my psychosis, and it had sort of become my alter-ego.

Caparosa was a young man, brilliantly creative, yet brilliantly disturbed. He was a master of the arts; a wonderfully creative writer, painter and songwriter. He also excelled in maths and sciences. He had the ability to break down any problem into workable parts and solve it. In him, was the key to life, love and happiness, as well as death, deception and greed. He was everything, to everyone. He was a world-class lover; a true romantic. He was a brilliant poet and an admired lyricist. He aimed for perfection in every aspect of his life. But, as the story that I invented in my psychotic state on the outside goes, once you attain perfection, there is nowhere else to go. Caparosa eventually attained complete and utter perfection, and at that exact moment in time, exploded. For, upon attaining true perfection, there is nowhere else to go. The mind needs to constantly better itself, to find new things to master. Therefore, if you master everything that there is, that leaves nothing else.

So J.T. would draw little pieces of art with this character in mind. I would talk for hours about Caparosa. To me, he was real. And to some extent, he became real to J.T. as well. We had an entire booklet of sketches and drawings with Caparosa as the central figure. I wrote out the lyrics to many of my songs for J.T. to gain inspiration from. Namely, the song *Caparosa*: *'I'm not here, you're crazy,'* rang the chorus. This song eventually became a staple of bands I played in years after. To this day, I still play it once in a while to remind myself of where my song writing began, and what I went through to get where I am now.

If we weren't chain-smoking in the smoking room or working on art concepts in the day room, we were doing 'the walk.' The walk was what we called our journey from one end of the giant hallway to the other. We knew exactly how many steps it took, and we would both touch the highly secured door before turning around and finishing the other leg of the walk. For hours, that was all we would do. When you are confined to such a small space, pacing comes naturally.

We made other friends on the ward as well. One was an older man in his seventies named Warren. He was extremely tall and in very good physical condition. I didn't know it, but my further psychiatric training leads me to believe that he suffered from dementia with psychotic features, likely due to Alzheimer's. He absolutely despised the nursing staff, as did J.T. and I. Therefore, we became allies. He would often put his arm around one of us and whisper 'don't let them get you alone,' or some other vague warning. He was always extremely pleasant to us, but whenever the nurses talked to him, a new side emerged. One day, J.T. and I sat back in awe as he took down five orderlies. A man in his seventies, taking down five men half his age. He was our new hero. He particularly took to J.T. and would often wrap his arm around him and offer his words of wisdom, ways of surviving captivity under the regime. On reflection now, I can see that he was quite ill, but back then, he was a great team mate. For the most part, he stuck to himself. But whenever Warren wanted to hang out, we were always happy to have him around.

There was another nice lady who became a dear friend to J.T. and I following our release. Her name was Debra and she was also in for major depression, as was J.T.. She was Native and had struggled against all odds to survive in a world where Native Canadians are perpetually given the short end of the stick. She had drug and alcohol issues, and was struggling to raise a young family. Her absolute warmth and kindness was a rare thing to find on the inside. J.T., Debra and I started spending more and more time together.

And there was also Joy, an older lady, perhaps in her middle sixties. She suffered from bipolar disorder and was in the grips of a wicked manic episode. She was always the happiest person on the unit, and would talk a mile a minute. And she was always knitting. Always. By the end of our stay there, J.T. and I both had more mittens and slippers than we would ever know what to do with.

Simply having a few familiar faces around made my stay much more tolerable. And by now, I was allowed to have visitors, only two at a time. J.T. and I had a way around that.

J.T. wasn't from the same town. He was from a small town a few hours away, and he didn't know many people in the city. I wanted to introduce my new best friend to my friends, so I would place a few phone calls and get a couple of friends to come visit. Two of them would say they were there to see me and two of them would say they were there to see J.T..

Visiting hours were what we both looked forward to the most. It was the only time that you could mentally distance yourself from the hell that was happening all around you.

Bridgette was my most frequent visitor. Since the second I met her at a party in The Ghetto, I was entranced. She was the most beautiful person I had ever known, and her kindness knew no bounds. She was with me through it all, and is the only friend who stayed with me the whole time and never faltered. During the months prior to being committed, we spent countless days together. She was the first, and only member of the 'Caparosa Cult.' She still holds on to that piece of paper that I made her sign during the grips of psychosis.

I knew she was special, and it turns out I was right. Eleven years after the fact, she is still a part of my life and has been a wonderful and supportive friend throughout the years following my admission to the hospital.

She would come and visit almost every single day. J.T. and I made it our mission to entertain her as much as possible, since we were so thankful to see anyone from the outside.

There was a ratty old guitar on the unit that we were able to sign out. When Brianne came to visit, we would set up camp in the smoking room and have a little concert. J.T. was a drummer, so he would concoct a makeshift drum set out of ashtrays and tables and play along. It probably wasn't a great scene for her, since the massive amounts of medication I was on made it extremely difficult to coordinate my guitar playing. But she didn't mind. Day after day, she would come. Our friendship grew, and she became fast friends with J.T. as well.

She would sometimes come solo, and sometimes with a few other friends. J.T. was always there, right by my side. Any friend of mine who visited, immediately became a friend of his, and he actually ended up dating one of my friends, while he was still locked in the psych. Needless to say, relationships that begin with one person locked in an asylum don't pan out that well, but it did last a few months, and it is certainly something hilarious to look back on when we get together.

Unfortunately, my 'progress' didn't last all that long. Whether it was the medication, which my mother believed it to be, or the sheer horrific surroundings, I once again ended up in a dark and violent place.

I attacked Clint again. I have a very, very vague recollection of this, so I won't go into great detail. All I recall is that we were playing pool and something went amiss. I went after him with the pool cue.

It was back to the bubble.

12

And Then There Were Voices

My next stint in the Bubble Room brought a whole new form of psychosis along with it. And for some reason, I am still able to recall it quite vividly. The mind tends to block out the most painful aspects of psychosis, but this memory has remained entrenched in my mind for years. I can still feel and recall those forty-eight hours as if they had just happened.

I was sitting on the cold, hard floor of the Bubble Room, but in my mind, I was sitting in a comfortable swivel-chair in the control room of a large radio station. I had a very expensive microphone hanging in front of my face, and across the mixing board sat two DJ's. I had finally made it. I was being interviewed on a national radio station. My words and my music would finally be heard by the world.

There was music blaring, people coming in and out of the control room. At first, they were just getting set up for the interview, so I sat back to take in my surroundings. They had pieces of paper all over the place and they kept on offering me coffee, tea, cappuccino, anything I wanted. It was a great feeling to finally be treated as the accomplished musician that I was. The respect that I felt I deserved was finally begin given to me.

With enough fair warning from the DJ's, the ON AIR sign came on. They began firing questions at me and I answered them as eloquently as I possibly could. I knew this was my big break. I didn't know what possible record producers were listening in, so I had to make a good impression. I made sure to not sound overly confident, but to also portray that I was a force to be reckoned in the music business.

They asked me about my childhood and my high school career. I went off on stories about how I used to play basketball but gave it all up once I discovered the guitar and the amazing power of composing music.

The imaginary interview went wonderfully. It seemed to go on for hours. I was on cloud nine. I was finally getting somewhere. Finally.

And then, out of the blue, reality caved in and broke me apart. I saw that I wasn't on a radio show at all. I was locked in a tiny, smelly, dark room in a psychiatric hospital. I simply *could not* permit this to be my reality.

I got up and started violently kicking the bubble as hard as I could. I would take runs at it, hitting it with every ounce of strength I had. It was shatterproof, so I stood no chance, but that didn't stop me from trying. I would run across the room, fly a foot into the bubble and then ram my head as hard as I could against the wall. Over, and over, and over.

Eventually, they came in - a team of the biggest orderlies and nurses. This time they had a special present for me that would keep me nice and safe and secure: a straightjacket.

I fought as hard as I could but they managed to get it on me. I screamed, kicked, punched, spat and bit them. I had just fallen deeper into a pit of unfathomable despair and I was not about to let them take me out without a fight.

It was designed in such a way to make it extremely difficult to stand up while wearing it, thus making it impossible to try to break the bubble. My arms were basically wrapped tightly around my torso. Everything was difficult wearing this fucking thing. However, after an intense struggle, I was able to figure out how to get on my feet by propping my back up against the wall. But every time I stood up, I would just go into a blind rage, ram myself into the wall and end up back on the floor. It became a vicious cycle, and I'm sure one that would have been horribly disturbing to watch.

It was extremely hard to navigate with this contraption. And to make matters worse for my coordination, I was given another injection at the same time that they applied the straightjacket. Now, not only was I locked in a psychiatric hospital, but I was locked in a room inside the psychiatric hospital and locked away from myself in a straightjacket. Without killing me, this was the most that they could possibly do to subdue me.

Until then, I hadn't been having audio and visual hallucinations. My psychosis was more based around delusions of grandeur and a belief in unnatural and impossible powers. The fact that I was now a part of an imaginary radio interview in which the participants were right in front of me, speaking to me, was a whole new ballgame.

When Dr. Dougson asked me to explain why I became increasingly violent in the Bubble Room when she showed up for work the next day, I explained the radio scenario to her. It just all seemed so fucking real. To this day, I can still picture the control room that we were sitting in. I can picture the radio hosts. I can still hear their voices if I really concentrate.

This new and unexpected symptom was cause for more medication. That was their answer for absolutely everything. Whatever they hadn't already tried on me was now on the agenda. I had a daily dose of over thirty different pills. Some for anxiety, some for depression, some for psychosis and some to just ensure that I didn't kill anyone. In legal terms, those types of sedatives are what qualifies as a 'medical restraint'. In theory, it is supposed to calm you down to the point that you don't require an actual straightjacket. For some reason, the medication seemed to have the opposite effect on me. Whatever new pills or injections they tried, I just fell further and further into a psychotic state.

Unfortunately, or fortunately, depending on how you look at it, that is the only hallucination that I recall well enough to describe here. I'm certain that it wasn't the only one. Since they had me on a new regimen of pills, my memory began to evade me. What I do know is that I spent at least the next week in and out of the Bubble Room for violent behaviour.

My educated guess would be that I would find myself in another hallucination and then upon realizing that it was not reality, I would lash out violently. That's what happened with the radio show, so I figure it's a fair assumption.

During this time, I once again wasn't allowed any visitors. I'm sure my mother and father must have been in an absolute panic, not knowing what was happening to me on the inside. It was for the best. No one who loved me should have seen me in that state. It was the type of thing that could haunt your memory for years. I was falling in and out of hallucinations, while constantly being trapped in my delusions. I still believed I was extremely prominent on the outside and was being held illegally. I believed that a helicopter would be coming to pick me up shortly. I believed that I had millions of dollars in an account on the outside. I believed that I had throngs of fans and admirers who just couldn't wait for me to be released from the unjust arm of the law. I was bigger than life. But only in my mind. In reality, I was a fucking lunatic on a rampage, with no hope of coming out of it anytime soon.

After about a week of violent outbursts and time spent in the bubble, I started to gain some sense of normalcy. Perhaps one aspect of the cocktail of medication was finally doing its job. I was once again allowed out in the ward but my Constant Observation would continue for a while yet.

They just couldn't trust me. My behaviour was so erratic and unpredictable that it was the only choice they had. They couldn't risk the bad publicity of one of their patients murdering another patient, or even a staff member. I was watched like a hawk, everywhere I went.

Even though I was on C.O. and definitely far, far from free, it felt great to be out again. J.T. and I got back to work on our drawings and our plans of world domination. I found out later that he was mostly humouring me, but for the most part, he went along with my delusions. He found them quite entertaining. My sheer enthusiasm for things that weren't real was enough to give him a break from his painful depression. My mental illness seemed to make his more bearable. Our time spent hanging out was a little more awkward now, seeing as I had a permanent staff 'friend' with me at all times. Depending on how I was acting, they would sometimes give us at least a few feet clearance to talk. Not that we were talking about anything all that important, but I certainly didn't want the staff to hear about my escape plan. After all, the helicopter should be coming any day now. If they got word that something was amiss, the jig would be up.

I spent a few days on Constant Observation and then was back to a regular ward citizen. Albeit, one with his own private room. That created some hostility among the other patients, but I really didn't care. I would just tell them that if they want their own room too, just attack everyone you see and be prepared to spend a lot of time in the bubble. In the end, they would realize that it wasn't quite worth it and that I had in fact earned my special treatment.

By then, I had been on the inside for about a month - a month and a half if you add in the two weeks at the General Hospital. For the first time since admission, the staff finally felt I was 'well' enough to participate in some of the therapeutic groups. I very vaguely remember them and certainly have no clue what the topics were. I do remember that I could never sit down long enough for the entire hour-long group. I would always be pacing back and forth behind the other patients. Typically, I would ask to leave early or they would ask me to leave as I was annoying the other patients with my constant pacing. Anything that required more than five seconds worth of attention at a time was impossible for me. My mind was rushing at a million miles per second and there was nothing that would slow it down. Typically, that's what the anti-psychotics are for. For some reason, they just didn't have the same effect on me. The madness would just have to run its course. A course that would take years to run.

A testament to just how drugged up I was can be found in a scenario that J.T. has always since found hilarious. I was given my nightly round of medication and went to bed. For some reason, the fire alarm had gone off. Although it turned out to be a false alarm, it went on for several minutes. I apparently didn't even move. A fire alarm. Couldn't. Wake. Me. Up.

13

BREATHING THAT SWEET OUTSIDE AIR

For the next week or so, things went along relatively smoothly. My delusions were still occurring, and would be for quite some time, but I was no longer displaying any violent tendencies. I was allowed to attend the groups, for as long as I could tolerate them, given my extreme level of anxiety, and I was even eventually given a Level Two. Level Two means that you are permitted to leave the unit, one on one, with a staff member. Having been locked in this tiny place for over a month, it was like winning the lottery. I still wasn't allowed to go outside, but simply getting past that locked door was enough for me for then.

Twice a day, I would get to walk around the hospital with a staff member. We would go to the canteen and I would stock up on chocolate bars and chips. There was even a used clothing store in the hospital. I ended up buying some of the most ridiculous clothes I had ever seen in my life. One particular shirt, the cloth equivalent of insanity, still hangs proudly in my closet. It's a mishmash of a million little boxes all of different colours. I wear it now to concerts sometimes and it serves as a great, silent reminder of where I've been. When people ask where I got it, I proudly reply 'a psych hospital!' which always immediately ends the conversation.

The privilege system works quite simply. You are given an inch, and expected to take only that inch. If you can handle that inch, you are then given an inch and a half. And so on. My privilege level was momentarily discontinued when one of the nurses spotted J.T. and I looking at the city bus schedule. We were deemed as an escape threat, and we both lost our levels.

With good behaviour, I was soon able to leave the ward again. And on top of that, I gained a Level Three. This allowed me to actually leave the hospital, and go outside. I had to be with a group of patients and a staff member had to be with us. The first time feeling that brisk winter air on my skin after so long inside a disinfectant hell was marvellous. Although we simply walked around the hospital grounds and smoked, it was like paradise. The risk of escape was pretty low, since the hospital was located in the middle of the woods, and grass went on for what seemed like miles. If you tried to run, they would simply drive out and pick you up. I wasn't even thinking of escape. When you are deprived of every possible freedom, any gain of freedom is magnificent. A few weeks prior, I was locked in a ward, and locked in a room, and locked in a straightjacket. Being able to walk around in the snow was almost like being born again.

This was a very confusing time for me. Although my delusions were still strong, they were beginning to come apart. I no longer believed that a helicopter would be coming to save me. I no longer believed that I was a world-famous musician. I no longer believed that my father was Satan incarnate. For the first time, I started to believe that maybe I had been a little insane. Maybe it isn't a grand conspiracy against me. Maybe there's a reason why every single person I knew believed I needed to be locked away from society.

I allowed my father to come and visit for the first time in months. He hadn't seen me and was relying solely on my mother's reports on my well-being. My father was and continues to be an outstanding person and although I'm sure he was hurt by my refusal to see him, I am also quite sure that he had the wherewithal to not take it personally. He knew more than anyone just how ill I was. My father is a brilliant man, one I respect immensely, and one that I am certainly happy to have a wonderful relationship with today.

My life began to have some sort of schedule, which was nice. We would go out for walks during the day, hit up the canteen. At night, friends and family would visit. I became quite close to J.T.'s mom as well as the families of some of the other patients. I was even somehow able to start an ill-fated romance with the cousin of one of the patients.

Her name was Sam. She had been visiting her cousin for as long as I had been on the inside. She got to witness me at my absolute worst, screaming at the top of my lungs from the Bubble Room. When I started to get better and was actually able to hold up my end of the conversation without veering off into convoluted conspiracy theories, I guess she saw something in me. I started to look forward to her visits. It was what got me through the day.

We continued our relationship briefly when I eventually got out. When again the depression took me over, I wasn't able to maintain a relationship with anyone, especially a romantic interest. We lost touch, which was probably for the best. As was witnessed with J.T. and my friend, psych hospitals are not the best places to start relationships. However, years later when we would sit around talking about our war stories, J.T. and I were always pretty impressed with ourselves that two lunatics were able to get girlfriends while being locked up. Trust me, it's no easy feat.

On the surface, things were getting better for me. But when it comes to mania, especially with psychotic features, better usually means worse; a different kind of worse. An inner worse. A turmoil only known to you, not visible from the outside.

It's a terrifying concept to lose a delusion or a hallucination. Something that just seems so real, that you would have bet your life on its existence, turns out to be a creation of your imagination. Just as you would grieve the death of a loved one, you begin to grieve the death of your delusions. It is somewhat comparable to waking up from a wonderful dream and then realizing that's all it was; a dream. But my dream had been going on for upwards of four months. It was going to take some time to accept the idea that nearly everything that I had thought was real, was in fact nothing. Nothing at all.

My symptoms started changing dramatically. For the treatment team, it was great news since I wasn't always talking about bizarre ideas, and was no longer lashing out physically. They viewed it as a step in the right direction. Instead, I was filled with unbelievable anxiety, depression and doubt. Upon slowly coming back to reality, the mind loses the ability to appreciate what has just happened. Once again, in a completely different way this time, nothing made any sense at all.

In technical terms, I would have been in a 'mixed-state' then. This simply means that you are experiencing some symptoms of mania, as well as some symptoms of depression and anxiety. But depression and mania can only coexist for so long. One needs to triumph over the other. I just wish someone would have tried to prepare me for what was to happen next.

The treatment team started talking about my release. But by then I no longer understood what release meant. A release to what? A release to all these horrible regrets and failed realizations? A release to world that I thought wasn't real? A release to what? What was beyond these walls?

Everything that I had known to be real had turned out to be false. Everything that I believed in, was in fact, nothing at all. It was a creation of my own imagination. What did they expect to release me to? I could barely sit still for more than thirty seconds, let alone go to a job interview. What did they want me to do?

My reality was no more. And the actual reality, that took the place of my psychotic reality, was in fact much more painful. I was to leave here, and somehow rejoin society? Knowing full well that my delusions were just that: delusions? Nothing that I thought happened actually happened? Here's your walking papers sir, have a good day. We sure hope you enjoyed your stay being crazy with us. Have a nice life.

No one on the treatment team really knew what to do with me. Not me, not my parents, not the doctors. It was thought that since drugs were what brought me there, it seemed to make sense that rehab would be a fitting next piece of the puzzle.

The paperwork was put through and I was next on the list for the 21-day inpatient drug and alcohol rehab facility in the centre of the city.

14

An Absolute Mental Horror Show

A nice way to end a story of early-onset psychosis would be to say that after being released, everything went back to normal. That everything was fine. But that would be a lie. It would be many years until things were ever 'fine' again.

I attended the three weeks of inpatient rehab. J.T. was there too, which made the transition much smoother. He got in a week before I did for his own addiction issues. It was a pleasant place, and much cleaner and less hospital smelling than what we were used to. The regimen was quite strict: everyone up at six AM and classes ran all day with homework in the evenings. There were breaks reserved during the day to talk to your specific counsellor. Too bad there wasn't a counsellor who was trained on what it was like to lose your entire mind at the age of 18. And there wasn't a counsellor on staff who could help you realize just what, in the fuck, had just happened to you.

All I got were formulaic answers about how drugs had done me wrong. No shit. Doing drugs is bad? Crazy news.

No matter how much I asked, no one could explain to me why I had just lost my mind completely for many, many months. No one could explain to me why I felt so defeated and alone. No one could tell me why

I felt like killing myself constantly. Nope. Just stay off drugs, and find the Lord.

I was already in the most confusing mental space that I have ever known, and was thrust into this bizarre world of 'religion for sanity.' Apparently, if I didn't accept God into my life, then there was no hope for me. I would be stuck forever in this wicked mess, for He was the only one who could save me.

I attended the lectures and completed the homework assignments, but never truly believed in this bizarre manner of rehabilitation from drug and alcohol dependence. I had always taken pride as a critical thinker, but my recent experiences in insanity had caused me to question my own thinking.

I was raised a church-going Catholic, but something just didn't add up in this place. I couldn't understand how religion was so entrenched in rehabilitation from drugs and alcohol. There definitely seemed to be a large piece of the puzzle missing.

I guess I had always had a problem with authority. Well, maybe not authority itself, but an authority that tried to get me to think the way they think, whether or not I believed it.

One of the many problems was that the counsellors there had no formal psychiatric training whatsoever. This was at a time when mental health and addictions were viewed and treated as separate ailments that had little to nothing to do with one another. To me, it seemed that it was impossible to treat one without treating the other. They were of little help in aiding my understanding of what had happened to me. And it didn't seem like there was much contact between the treatment team at the hospital and the one at rehab. Thankfully, we are now seeing a change in the way that mental health and addictions treatments are offered. They are viewed as two parts to a whole now. You cannot treat one without treating the other, which makes sense. At the time, that was a foreign concept. It was Jesus or nothing.

This didn't turn out to be a healthy way for me to begin my freedom. Instead of answering the many questions I had been left with from the hospital and everything leading up to it, I was left with even more questions. I was plunged into a world that didn't make sense. These so-called professionals preaching answers to me that I knew to be false. I certainly wasn't the genius I believed myself to be in my psychotic state, but I could still see through the bullshit that they were preaching to me. I just ended up more confused, more lost, and much, much more alone.

One positive thing did happen while I was there. I didn't realize it until looking back with a clear head, but it was then that I decided what I wanted to do with my life. Being fed up with the simpleton advice that I was begin given by the counsellors, I told myself that I, one day, would be on the other side of the desk. As should be expected, when I told the counsellors of this goal, they labelled it as 'grandiose thinking' which was something that they needed to curb. Instead of supporting me in a dream that could help me better myself by helping others, they stifled it and insisted that it was a terrible idea.

The idea was still ingrained in me. Albeit, it would be another ten years until I led my first concurrent disorders group with patients with severe psychotic illnesses and comorbid drug addictions, but the seed was planted during that stint in rehab.

Clearly, I was in no position to start the necessary schooling to become a counsellor. Although I wasn't necessarily insane anymore, I wasn't quite sane either. I was a mess. An absolute mental horror show.

I had my birthday in rehab that year. I turned nineteen, the legal drinking age in Canada, in rehab. J.T.'s mom brought me a cake, but I wasn't allowed to have it. She might have snuck drugs into it.

Three weeks later, I was released from rehab. I was finally fully free. Weekly appointments with a psychiatrist were now my only contact with the system. Other than that, I was left to my own devices. Which, it turns out, weren't particularly strong.

My parents, still, after all of this, being the wonderful, loving and caring people that they are, took me in. It was time to start the road to recovery. The most beaten, run down and ragged road that could ever exist.

15

INSANE'S THE NEW SANE

Our mental health system works in a weird and frightening manner. Unless your behaviours are severely disturbing other people and causing risk to yourself and others, you are basically asked to figure it out for yourself. Sure, I had a psychiatrist, but he was more like a drug dealer than a therapist. Every week, he would ask me the same formulaic questions about appetite, mood, anxiety, sleep, interests and then either increase my medication, or try something new. He never really tried to get behind the feelings. He didn't care to figure out where they came from. He just wanted to quash them with drugs. I was left alone to figure out what had happened to me. Which was fucking terrifying.

Every possible option raced through my head. Maybe I had bipolar disorder. Maybe, I was going to have a psychotic break like this every few months. Maybe the rest of my life will never be normal. Maybe I will be in and out of psychiatric hospitals until one day I die in one. Or, I die at my own hand. Or, even worse, maybe I have schizophrenia. The first episode of schizophrenia usually hits around age 18. I tried hard to convince myself that it was just the drugs that landed me there, but it was really hard to say. Since my psychiatrists in the hospital couldn't diagnose me, and my psychiatrist out of the hospital couldn't diagnose me, I just feared the worst.

I did as much research as I could. Since my mind was still quite scattered and my anxiety was through the roof, it was hard to focus. And, as I later learned, research into drug induced psychosis was still in its infancy. At the time, the medical professionals didn't really believe that drugs on their own could cause psychosis. It always had to be part of a larger problem, such as bipolar disorder, schizophrenia, or schizoaffective disorder, which is basically a combination of the two. My research never led in a promising direction. It only furthered my belief that the rest of my life was barely going to be worth living. The depression worsened. The anxiety became stifling, which only led me to believe even more that I was suffering from one of these debilitating, life-long mental illnesses.

J.T. and I spent a lot of time together that summer. I felt as though he was the only one I could really talk to. It was as if my other friends from before no longer knew who I was, for who I was had changed quite dramatically. He was going through much of the same as I. He didn't have a diagnosis; didn't know what the hell was wrong with him. One day, we were talking on the phone and we both said at basically the same time that we felt empty. There was no other word for it. Complete and utter emptiness. Like everything inside had been Robbed from us. That we were only part human now. We had forgotten what it was like to feel. There was nothing, but emptiness. And since we were both sworn off of alcohol and drugs, there was nothing to fill that void. Just day, after day, after day of feeling enormously defeated and alone. Even in a crowded room at a party, I felt utterly and completely alone. I even felt alone when I was with J.T., but it was a comfortable aloneness, since I knew that he felt it too. We didn't have to explain ourselves to one another. We just knew.

Feeling this way makes it really hard to resume a social life. There is nothing more difficult in the world than pretending that you aren't depressed; pretending that you have some hope for the future; pretending that you give a shit about some mundane conversation you are having with an acquaintance. My social interactions were always time limited. I would still go to parties and see friends, but I wouldn't drink or do drugs, would barely talk to anyone and would leave usually after an hour or so.

My anxiety was just through the roof and I could no longer handle social situations. I did ok one on one, depending on the person. But that person also had to be ok with the fact that there might be extended periods of awkward silences in our conversations. I often just didn't have the words. I was lost in a world of loneliness and confusion and doubt.

One of the hardest things to come to terms with was the fact that I was not a successful musician. Well, at least not on the terms that my delusion had created. I had recorded a CD which was enjoyed by many people, but that accomplishment no longer felt like anything meaningful. But I tried. I tried so fucking hard to get back into music. It had been months since I had been able to play and my skills had suffered greatly. My singing voice was no longer the one that was on the CD, regardless of the fact that I had recorded the CD at the high point of my insanity. I believed that the world was watching me, and it showed in my voice. The thing about singing is that if you don't have the confidence to pull it off, even if you have a good voice, it's not going to work. Confidence was something that I had none of. I went from being the most confident person that anyone had ever seen, to someone who doubted every single talent that I once had.

Many nights were spent in my parents' basement playing the CD and singing along, but I would do so quietly. I didn't even have the confidence for my parents to hear my singing voice anymore. I kept at it. I knew I loved music. I knew I loved writing and creating music, and I just wasn't about to let that die. I am thankful for that today. Although I am still not what one would consider a widely successful recording artist, I have been able to amass a few local 'hits' and recorded some music videos, also dealing with my experiences in mental confusion. That came to be many years later. During the first year after psychosis, no one besides my parents heard my music, and they only heard the whispered versions. Fortunately it was something that I still had, and that I just could not let go of.

J.T. had his artwork and his poetry and I had my music. It was all we had to help us through these terrible times. Some semblance of hope for the future, and if not that, at least a creative outlet to let out our horrible confusion and despair.

Things sort of crept along like this for about four months. I spent my time mostly alone, deep in thought, savagely depressed and acutely anxious. I spent a lot of time with J.T.. We drank pot upon pot of coffee and chain smoked cigarettes. We hung out with some people we had met in rehab. It seemed like life had come to a halt. I really didn't know where to go from here.

One day, J.T. and I were hanging out, drinking coffee and smoking cigarettes. The topic of drinking came up. We both found it sort of funny that even if we wanted to start drinking again, we couldn't, since both of our families as well as our large group of mutual friends would have nothing of it. We both still felt empty. Still. After many months, there was no word for it other than empty. We wanted to feel alive again. We just wanted to feel something, anything, but pain. But we couldn't do it there.

Fairly soon after the topic was broached, it was decided: we were going to hitchhike to J.T.'s hometown and get absolutely shit tank wasted. It was the only place that we could do it unnoticed. And the next day, we left.

It wasn't a long trip, just about a two hour drive from where we were living, so we headed out around noon. We started walking out of the city limits on the highway, assuming that we would get picked up fairly soon. This was my first hitching adventure, but J.T. was an esteemed veteran. He assured me that it would not take long to be picked up. Three hours later, we were getting near the psych hospital, where we had both been both locked up only a few months prior. We laughed at the irony of how we had fucked ourselves, since no one will pick up a hitchhiker near a psych hospital. But, being past the point of turning back, we just kept walking. It was another few hours until we were far enough away from the hospital so that people wouldn't immediately think that we were escapees. We finally got picked up.

J.T. sat in the front, since I was quite clear of the fact that I could not hold up a conversation with a stranger. The guy was about our age and absolutely adored rave music, blasting it as loud as his speakers would allow. And since we were his grateful passengers, we did not complain. It was awful. There isn't much in the world that I hate more than rave music, but this fellow was giving us a ride right to J.T.'s hometown, and thus, we were happy. It would only be a short while before we could forget what had happened to us over the past six months by breaking our brains with booze.

We got to town and I quickly learned what kind of guy J.T. had been before I met him. We went to his pal's place, which was littered with booze bottles, bongs and violence. J.T. had played drums in a metal band with the guys who lived here, prior to being sent to the psych hospital, and these guys were as metal as they come. They would repeatedly punch each other in the face as hard as they could. It was some sort of weird game. At first, J.T. sort of acted aloof, as if this was something that he didn't partake in…until after we got back from the liquor store.

J.T. and I got a case of beer and some whiskey, clinked our glasses, and let loose. Within an hour, J.T. was punching his friends as hard as he could and I was just hoping that I wouldn't end up involved in this violent manner of friendship. As the new guy, they didn't make me partake in the violence. Even the drinking in itself was violent. For two people who had recently lost their minds, and had then stayed sober for many months after that, there was a lot of letting loose and letting go that night. In truth, we had a blast. It felt good to feel something again. It was the first time I had had fun in months, the first time that I felt like a real person again. It also helped that his friends did not know me, did not know my story, so I had nothing to hide. I could be whoever I wanted to be. I finally felt free again. I no longer felt empty.

We hitched back home the next day, feeling somewhat rejuvenated, also faced with the problem of whether to tell our friends of what we had done, or to keep it a secret. We decided to tell them. Point blank. We're drinking again. So, deal with it.

I guess I didn't realize the level of J.T.'s alcoholism. It sort of took him over right from the start. I indulged with friends around the campfire, but J.T. took it to a new level. One night, a few of our friends were having some drinks and barbecue around the fire and J.T. had a little too much. He disappeared, which had become a normal occurrence for him. He would just go on random solo drunken adventures through the neighbourhood while the rest of us stayed back and sipped beers by the flames. I didn't hear from him the next day, and the day after that, my parents told me what happened to him. They had read it in the paper, and they were not impressed.

In his drunken stupor, he had broken into a marina and was quickly spotted by an employee and subsequently arrested by the police for breaking and entering. Upon reading the story in the newspaper, my parents assumed that I had also been a part of the crime, but that I had just managed to escape in time. Although that was a pretty believable way of interpreting things, I actually had nothing to do with it. I didn't know what had happened to him that night. Now, thanks to the news media, I knew that he was being held in jail.

I went to visit him in jail. Although we had met in a highly secured psychiatric hospital, jail was a whole new realm. It was a creepy place. I feared that this was the place I was going to eventually end up. I signed some documents, was searched by an officer and eventually led into a room with a huge plate of glass in front of it. I sat awkwardly where I was told as I eavesdropped on other visitors' conversations with their boyfriends, sons, husbands and brothers. All of a sudden, there he was. He appeared in front of me, decked out in a full orange jumpsuit. He had a smile on his face, but I knew it was for my benefit only. How anyone could have a smile in this place was beyond me.

Normally, you wouldn't be held in jail for a simple B&E charge, but J.T. had outstanding charges. It wasn't really something that we ever spoke about, although I'm sure it was something that was constantly on his mind. Now that they had him in custody, he would have to face the consequences of his other charges, ranging from mischief, to theft, to other B&Es. J.T. had led quite the life before we had met.

I didn't really even know what to ask him. The only thing that made sense was 'how long, man?' The answer was, he didn't really know. Since he didn't have any money, he would be getting a court-appointed lawyer. And since those lawyers have to try several cases a day, for minimal pay, it was almost assured that they wouldn't be putting a hell of a lot of effort into any one specific case. I left the prison feeling just awful. One minute we were hanging out and having a good time by the fire and the next, he's decked in orange, identified by a number and unaware of when he will get to see the clear blue sky.

It was weird now. I felt terrible for J.T., but I also felt terrible because I no longer had my confidant. I felt selfish even thinking that. How could I say that his being incarcerated was a problem for me? I still had my freedom. J.T. had nothing. It felt incredibly selfish to feel this way. So, I did all that I could and visited him as much as was allowed.

Thankfully, he did alright on the inside. J.T. had a certain survival instinct in him that not many people have. He was able to adapt to even the most horrendous situations. He did his best to make the best of the cards he had been dealt, and I admired him for this.

After a few weeks, he was released. His lawyer had managed to find a way to get him out until he was brought to trial for his crimes.

16

PSYCHIATRIC LIMBO

I couldn't handle it anymore. I needed to do something with my life. I couldn't handle being in psychiatric limbo any longer. I started looking into options of escaping the devastating mental torment I was in.

The only option seemed to be school. I had fucked up school in the biggest way possible so I thought it apt to try again. Since I was banned from the college in my hometown, I would have to go elsewhere. I started researching programs at other colleges in other cities. And since journalism and writing had been the only thing that I knew I was good at, I figured I would try that again. I found a college two hours away that would accept me. And my parents, who also wondered how in the hell I would go on with my life after all of this, were more than happy to pay for it.

So, in September, I moved a few hours down the road for my second attempt at post-secondary education. J.T. had decided to go on a hitchhiking journey across the country, a journey that he tried to convince me to participate in, but I guess I knew it would be a bad idea. I no longer wanted to run from my problems. I wanted to put all this shit behind me and start over. Life had other things in store for me.

My parents had agreed to fund my next journey but certainly didn't want to break the bank. We went to check out the city and find me a place to live. After checking out a few disastrous rooms, we found a place that was affordable and seemed quite nice at the time. We didn't know it then, as the area was unfamiliar to us, but it was in the worst part of town. The absolute worst. During the day, it just seemed like any other part of town. There was a burger joint down the street, a Laundromat within walking distance and a convenience store. It seemed fine. It was a room in an apartment with two other students who seemed like upstanding citizens.

I started the journalism program, again. I didn't let any of the other students or profs know that I had already been kicked out of a journalism program. And naturally, I didn't let them know that I'd been recently locked up in a highly secured psychiatric hospital.

The first few months went alright. Again though, I didn't feel challenged. Having been raised by a respected national journalist as a father, the methods they taught me in school were rudimentary at best. I knew how to write a lead. I knew how to interview people. I knew how to scope out a story. I guess, after the first two months or so, I got bored.

One Friday night at the apartment, I decided to get wasted and play some music. By then, I had begun to gain some confidence in my singing and song writing ability again. I got a bottle of gin and busted out the guitar on the back porch. I had a great time. A few of the neighbours came out and told me how much they loved it when I played music. It sort of gave me the boost I needed. One neighbour, Travis, stopped by to tell me how much he enjoyed the music. He invited me over to his place for a party.

He was about my age, and loved to drink. He wasn't in school, and in fact, hadn't even graduated high school, but I was hard pressed for friends. I was only a shell of a human being and this guy who lived in my neighborhood and had a cool dog seemed like an appropriate friend choice. Not a lot of thinking involved. I didn't expect him to ever want to talk about one another's feelings. He was, as you might say, a little rough around the edges.

We started to hang out. My social skills were still extremely raw, but he was a simpleton who was easy to get along with. He became someone to pass the time with. I knew of his criminal past as he didn't try to hide it from anyone. He fought a lot, and Robbed a lot.

I would hang out at his apartment on weekends and his friends would come over and regale us with stories of their armed Robberies, counterfeiting schemes and break and enters. I think I knew that I was certainly hanging with the wrong crowd, but it felt good to be among people who didn't know my past. They actually respected me quite a bit, for I was the 'smart' one of the group. They were in all reality, a group of low-life criminals. But coming from where I had just been, that didn't matter to me. I weirdly identified with them.

One day, Travis showed up at my apartment. He said he needed money for booze. I was broke at the time so he asked me if he could pawn my stereo. I had a pretty nice stereo system. I said no. No fucking way. He came back an hour later with his buddy Tattoo, and they took my stereo.

He Robbed me. I didn't know what to do with this information. I couldn't confront him, because he was twice my size and all his friends were street level thugs who would have me down on the ground within seconds. But I was enraged with the fact that he had taken my stereo. After debating on what to do for hours, I called the cops and reported him.

Apparently, from what I heard later, the cops brought him in but there was no hard evidence, since he had pawned the stereo already, and he was let go. So, I was now left with this raging asshole who had the knowledge that I had called the cops on him. The next night brought with it a turn of events that would leave a great physical and mental mark on the rest of my life.

I was heading down to the convenience store in the neighbourhood when Travis and his buddy Tattoo confronted me. Travis pretended that everything was fine. He said he was really sorry for stealing my stereo, that he would repay me. He felt really bad about it and really wanted to make amends. He told me to come to Tattoo's house to have a drink to repay me with. Although I was suspicious, I knew I really didn't have a choice in the matter. What was going to happen, was going to happen no matter what I did. I was fucked. I could have run, and been caught and beaten immediately, or gone with them, and hope to talk myself out of the beating. I decided to go with them and hope to be able to talk myself out of what was about to happen. Because the truth was, he *had* stolen my stereo. I was the one who should be mad here, not him. I was unfamiliar with how things went down in the ghetto. I was now a Rat.

Tattoo was a career criminal, covered head to toe in tattoos. Even on his face. He's the kind of person that if you saw on the street, you would assume either just got released from jail or was just on his way to jail. He meant business, and was also a drug dealer. I didn't get involved with drugs after what they had done to me before, but I was very much aware of what he did for a living and the people he hurt. I knew he wasn't someone I wanted on my bad sad, but it was far too late.

The three of us sat around awkwardly at Tattoo's place. Travis kept on saying that there was no ill will between us, but I knew that this was bullshit. We had a few drinks and I just hoped that I was going to get out of there alive.

Late into the night, we all stepped out into the backyard for a smoke. I knew something was up. I could just sense it. As I stood there puffing on a cigarette, Travis screamed at me.

"You fucking rat!"

He ran at me and pummelled me in the face as hard as he could with both his fists. I immediately fell to the ground. He proceeded to kick me and punch me in the face as hard as he could. There was nothing I could do. I took the beating. He hit me as hard as possible, all the while screaming that I was a 'fucking rat piece of shit.'

For the first few seconds of the beating, Tattoo just stood there watching and smoking. Watching and smoking.

After about thirty seconds of me getting savagely kicked and punched while lying on the ground defenceless, Tattoo intervened and pulled Travis off of me. He told me to run, and I did. I ran as fast as I fucking could. I ran all the way back to my apartment and locked the door.

It took a while to process what had actually happened to me. Waking up the next morning and seeing my face in the mirror certainly helped to make it more real. One entire side of my face was a combination of black, blue and red. Both eyes black. I looked awful, and felt twenty times worse than I looked.

We were laying out the journalism department's newspaper that day, so I didn't have a choice but to go to class. When I walked into the newsroom, all eyes were on me. People I had never even spoken to were coming up to me and asking what had happened. Upon recounting the story time after time, people showed some genuine sympathy for me. I had many offers of couches to crash on and many hands offering to help me move out of that disturbing part of town.

I was now fairly terrified of Travis, and I didn't think that his wrath of pain was going to stop anytime soon. I was no longer safe at home. He could show up at any time, just to let off some more steam on my face. My classmate Mark offered for me to spend a few nights at his apartment on the other side of town, which was greatly appreciated. He lived near the school, which was a part of town that I knew I would never see Travis in. He abhorred the thought of higher learning, probably because it scared the living crap out of him.

I had a friend named Helen who lived in residence who also offered me the use of their living room sofa bed any time I needed it. There were six girls living there, all of whom I had become decent friends with, so it was a comfortable place to be, and safe. After spending a few nights with Mark, I basically moved into Helen's living room. It was in that living room that seemingly, things were about to start getting better for the first time.

It was a typical Friday night in a college dorm. A bunch of people were over, hanging out and drinking beer in the living room and the girls were in and out of Helen's room and the bathroom trying out various hair and makeup options, getting ready for the bar. I wasn't planning on going out with them, since they tended to frequent dance bars, which typically stand for everything that I am against in this world. The music is terrible, you have to shout to have a conversation, douchebags are gyrating everywhere and on everything and there are usually fights outside.

Everything changed when Shannon came to the door. I'd go to a dance bar with her any day. I had just never seen anyone like her before. She was nearly as tall as me, topping out around 5'9 and had the body of a Hollywood starlet. Her hair was a long, perfectly blended mix of brown and blonde with various other coloured highlights that just accentuated her gorgeous facial features. Her smile was one of the most beautiful things I had ever seen. Suddenly, I had an overwhelming desire to go to the dance bar with them.

Typically, upon meeting someone who possesses that rare form of perfect beauty, it is only a matter of time until I find some horrible flaw that would render the person un-datable. Intelligence, or lack thereof, tends to be a deal-breaker for me. I can look past most things in a partner, but if someone cannot hold up their end of a conversation, their beauty quickly loses its appeal. I found I didn't have to worry about that with Shannon. She was an English major at the University across town and shared the same passion for words as I. She was quick-witted, extremely interesting and a very engaging conversationalist.

There was still one fairly large problem. She was currently living with her boyfriend from high school who had moved to town with her when she started University. Things weren't going well, to say the least. He was unemployed, drinking heavily and being both verbally and physically abusive towards her. Not typically one to try to steal someone's girlfriend away, this douchebag made it an apt thing to consider. This guy clearly didn't realize what he had, and with the way she was telling me he treated her, I knew he didn't deserve to be with her any longer. I had my heart set on Shannon, and made it my mission to save her from this wicked monster of a human she was living with.

It certainly wasn't easy - for anyone involved; by the time we had come back from Christmas holidays her boyfriend had moved out and I had taken his place. There were a few occasions when things almost came to blows between he and I. That definitely wouldn't have worked out well for me since he was a muscular hockey playing type and I was a skinny guitar playing type. But thankfully Shannon was always able to interject and keep him from beating me into the ground.

I had done it. I had ousted the ruling dictator and assumed his throne, and his bed. It's amazing the things you can do under the duress of love.

Shannon had a very nice one bedroom apartment in the West end of the city. It wasn't anywhere near Travis and was in a part of town completely unknown to me. It was like starting completely anew. And the first time I had ever lived with a girlfriend.

Although it didn't seem odd to her or I, I'm sure a lot of people thought it was a terrible idea. After all, we met, ousted her boyfriend, and moved in together all within the space of a month. But after what had happened to me in recent times, I no longer held much of a grasp of normality. I needed a place to live and she needed to get rid of her boyfriend. It made perfect sense.

It was a great feeling being constantly surrounded by someone you love. I likely thought at the time that this was how I was going to spend the rest of my life, and I couldn't have been more pleased about it. Just like all good things thus far in my life, it couldn't last.

17

SOMETHING OF A DARKER SHADE

I made a classic writer's mistake. I decided to try and start writing about my experience of completely losing my mind long before I was fully able to comprehend it. It was still a huge part of my life and dominated much of my thinking. I talked to Shannon about it often and I think it freaked her out. It would freak anyone out.

I still wasn't really sure about anything, especially feelings. But I thought that if I put what happened onto paper, then I could be done with it. That I could move on. Not enough time had passed. Not even close to enough time had passed.

What you are reading now is about the fifth from-scratch attempt at putting this story into words. I guess perhaps eleven years is how long you should wait before putting a horrible memory onto paper.

Shannon had this old typewriter for some reason, so we set that up on the dining room table. We would share her computer to do school work and whatnot, and I would work on the story on this vintage typewriter. It felt right to be writing on something so archaic. There was certainly something raw and savage about it. The words that I planned on writing would be just as savage, so I figured it to be a perfect fit, not knowing that this simple writing project would be a major contributing cause of my next mental demise.

A few weeks into living together, our true selves started to shine through. Since we had moved in together during the infatuation phase, we had to go through the 'reality-sets-in-phase' whilst living together. Shannon had been with the guy prior for basically her entire dating life. They were high school sweethearts. Even though he ended up being mean and abusive in the end, it didn't make it any easier on her. But it wasn't just the break up that was bothering her. I could sense that there was something much deeper happening inside of this beautiful girl. Something of a darker shade that completely contradicted her bright and shining affect. Her deep anxiety was beginning to control her in every single way.

I didn't know what else to do, so I just tried to put the words onto paper, which is a really hard thing to do when you still don't quite comprehend what happened. I would stay up all night writing and then spend the days contemplating what I was writing, and what exactly had happened. I still didn't know. I was trying to write a story that didn't have an ending. The story was still being written. It was still being lived.

Shannon quickly became anxiety ridden. Going to class was hard for her; going to work was even harder. She was worried about everything. Every single thing a person could worry about. As her worry caused her to do things such as miss class or work, she would then worry more as a result. It was a vicious cycle.

As her anxiety worsened, my depression grew. I would often stay up all night writing, and then sleep all day. I would spend any time awake just pondering and reconstructing and attempting to understand what had happened to me just months prior. I knew if I could put it into words in my head, I could put it into words on paper.

When two people with worsening mental states live together in a relatively small apartment, things can get very, very bad. My depression made her anxiety much worse. Her anxiety made my depression much worse. We both only wanted to help each other, but neither one of us knew how to help ourselves.

School became a thing of the past for both of us. Even though Shannon had a car, it was too much of a mental and emotional challenge for either of us to embark on. We didn't admit we were dropping out though. We kept some form of hope alive, occasionally handing in assignments. I thought I could recover my semester. And I probably could have, had I been sane.

School became less and less important. The thing with depression is that it causes everything to become less important. Sure, finishing school would be great. On the other hand, why does it matter if you're just going to kill yourself anyway?

My depression didn't waste any time. It went from mild to insanity in only a few weeks.

I eventually stopped trying to write the story. My mental condition had deteriorated to a point where I couldn't even focus on anything for any long period of time. And there was nothing to be written. I was defeated, and obviously still within the thrusts of the story. I would spend my time on the typewriter writing Shannon five and ten page letters. Even though we lived together and talked all the time, I just never felt that I was able to get it all out with the spoken word. I don't know, and don't want to know, what was written in those letters, but I know it was probably painful to read. I think I was trying to explain myself to her. Trying to explain what was happening to me. Trying to understand what was happening to her.

I wrote poems and lyrics on the typewriter as well. A few songs came out of that apartment but none that have lasted for any period of time. For some, depression can be inspiring. For others, it can be debilitating. For me, I guess it was a combination. I could still be artistic in some way, but my art would come out just as distorted and depressed as I was, so it certainly wasn't appealing to anyone else. But I wasn't writing or making music for anyone else, I was doing it for me. There just had to be some way to get all these unfamiliar feelings and emotional anguish out of my mind and into some other medium.

Things really came to a head one particular night. It wasn't a night any different than any other; nothing different had happened. Shannon left to her evening shift and I stayed back in the apartment. But I guess it had just been boiling up for too long. Something had to give. I needed out of my mind.

Shannon had a bottle of rum tucked away for a special occasion. I thought that it would provide some peace of mind or at least dull me to the point of being able to tolerate it. Clearly that is an extremely statistically unfounded hope. Of course it would make it worse. Alcohol is a depressant, simple as that. It depresses the central nervous system, and is thus the absolute worst idea in the world if you are depressed. I know that now. I didn't know it then, or if I did, I at least didn't want to admit it to myself. I needed to get out of my brain.

I poured myself a stiff rum and Coke. It was basically 80% rum, 20% Coke. It went down like water, and so did the next one, and the one after that. I sat in front of the typewriter chain-smoking and chain-drinking and trying to write something.

I ended up back in the kitchen to fix myself another drink and noticed the large butcher's knife that Shannon had hanging against the wall. It didn't even seem like a conscious decision at the time. I picked it up. Held it. Stared at it. Admired how powerful and destructive it could be. I wondered what I could do with it.

I went back to the typewriter, by now quite impaired, and tried to write a letter to Shannon. I don't remember the contents of the letter, but I'm sure it was a thinly veiled apology for what I was about to do next. But I didn't know what I was about to do next.

The alcohol just wasn't doing its part in blocking out the pain. I needed something more. I had some extremely powerful sleeping pills left over from my last battle with madness. I figured adding a few of those into the mix couldn't be a bad idea.

Even when taken without alcohol, anything more than the recommended dose of these things causes you to black out and behave as a disastrous drunk. I have no idea how many I took that night.

Saturated with so much alcohol, the pills didn't take long to kick in. Much of what happened next is a scrambled mess in my memory. What I know for sure is that I went back to the kitchen and grabbed the knife. I had the decency at least to go into the bathroom. Over the sink, I started to rub the extremely sharp knife against the skin of my left arm. I wasn't planning on killing myself. If I was, I would have come up with a much more definitive measure than wrist cutting. Although it can work, it is extremely rare that it does, and it requires a great amount of dedication in order to complete the task. I didn't want to die, at least not then, I just didn't want to feel like this any longer. I wanted an escape. I wanted out of my own mind.

I ran the blade up and down my arm, making small superficial cuts all along. I watched the blood drip from my arm and cascade beautifully into the sink. As I did it, a sense of calm enveloped me. It was the perfect release. Well, it may have been the perfect release had I been able to stop there.

I could not stop there. I had to continue.

The cuts got worse and worse, and the pills and the booze took me over even more. Although I don't recall doing this, I know that I called 911 at some point. The rest of what happened has had to be told back to me by Shannon, for I was in a completely blacked-out state.

I apparently stayed on the phone with the 911 operator the entire time. I have no idea what I put that poor person through, but I can only imagine that it was less than pleasant. When two police officers knocked on my door, I reacted with pure psychotic panic. I tried to attack them. In doing so, I ended up smashing my head against the concrete wall in our apartment entrance. I was certainly in no state to attack anyone and likely simply lunged at them and fell on my own, which is why they didn't try to charge me with assaulting a police officer. Had it been two different officers having a bad day, my entire future could have been decided that night. As they were fully aware that I was in a very disturbed emotional state, they did their best to help me and to get me to a hospital. The ambulance arrived shortly after and the paramedics tended to my self-inflicted wounds as well as the wound on my head after ramming it into concrete. I was taken away in an ambulance to the hospital.

Shannon got home from work apparently shortly after I was taken away. Our landlord quickly brought her up to date on what had happened, or at least what he had seen. From his perspective, her drunk and bloodied boyfriend had tried to assault police officers.

I guess I had told the operator that my girlfriend would be coming home soon. As these were the days before cell phones were commonplace, she took it upon herself to keep calling the apartment after I was taken away, until Shannon finally picked up the phone.

The operator explained to Shannon what had happened. How I had ingested alcohol and sleeping pills and self-administered several cuts to my arm and wrists. She let her know where she could find me.

That poor, poor girl. Like she didn't have enough to deal with.

I was only kept in the hospital overnight. I was evaluated by a psychiatrist in the morning and he deemed me not as a threat to myself and let me go. Upon returning home the next day, the horrible situation that I was already in became exponentially worse. While I was at the hospital, Shannon had uncovered some of my journal writings. They detailed my regret at getting involved with her in the first place and spoke of how my true and undying love was Jennifer, the one who had gotten away. She was not pleased.

My list of problems just kept getting bigger and bigger. No one at the hospital had thought that maybe I required some form of counselling or something, they just let me loose, back into my wretched depression that was now compounded by an angry and already extremely anxious girlfriend.

I can't even imagine, looking back, what I did to Shannon's mental health during that time. She was already having a hard time, then I come into her life, leave her bathroom a bloody, psychotic mess while she finds out that my love still lies with my ex-girlfriend.

The next while living together was absolutely disastrous. Since my encounter with the medical professionals did nothing to help me, my mental condition continued to deteriorate. And now, not only was I faced with the demons created in my mind, I had real-life problems as well. My girlfriend no longer trusted me alone; I had all but failed out of school; I had nothing going for me. Nothing. Again.

We fought constantly. It became the only thing either of us was capable of. We fought about my ex-girlfriend and we fought about her ex-boyfriend. We fought about every single thing that any two people could fight about it. As quickly as it had come, the magic had disappeared. Little over four months into our relationship and things had completely deteriorated into a disastrous mess.

Both of our school years were now officially fucked. We were just two people, from different cities, living in a strange city that was new to both of us. Neither of us knew why were even there anymore. It obviously wasn't working, and was only making both of us worse.

We tried to break up. Both of us were so emotionally attached to the other that it was impossible. We were both in psychiatric crisis.

18

RUNNING FROM A DREAM

I'm not proud of what happened next. In my entire history of bad things that I have done, this takes the cake.

During one of our extended arguments I had told Shannon that I didn't even see the point in me being in this city any longer. I came here for school, which I had failed out of, and our relationship obviously wasn't working. But she didn't have anywhere to go. Her parents were going through an incredibly painful divorce and moving back to her hometown was just not an option.

I selfishly created my own option.

My band mates from high school had since moved to Ottawa, Ontario, the capital city of Canada. I figured that was where I should escape to. I could go back to making music, the only thing that made sense to me throughout these turbulent years.

One day while Shannon was at work, I packed whatever little belongings I had into a few small bags, grabbed my guitar and hopped a bus to Ottawa. I left Shannon a note telling her sorry I was, but that this was how it had to be. A definite low point of my life, but it happened.

I got to Ottawa late that evening and by the time I had arrived at my band members' apartment, she had already figured out where I was. The first thing my lead guitar player Kent said when I walked in the door was "Shannon just called here man. She knows what's up."

The first night, I just tried to enjoy myself and forget about all the problems that had been following me for the past several years. But by the next day, I had to give in and talk to her. She was obviously very mad, but not really all that surprised. She could tell for some time that something was up with me and that something drastic was about to happen. She probably didn't think I would move six hundred kilometres away while she was at work, but she knew *something* was going to happen.

We talked, and talked. It was true, I still did love her. The passion I had felt when I met her was not an illusion. She was truly an amazing and remarkable person, but things just weren't working out. We were both crazy, although I didn't use those words. Within less than a week, we agreed that we needed to see one another and that she would come to Ottawa for a weekend.

Maybe it was just a change of scenery that we needed. We had met shortly after I had had my face pummelled in, and during her painful extrication of her ex-boyfriend. The new city seemed to work. We were all over each other like we were in the beginning. Shannon ended up spending a few days in our apartment, which ended up not making me very popular among my band mates. My bedroom was right next to Kent's and he had to listen to us every night, and every morning, and every afternoon.

All of a sudden, it was like we were back at the start of our relationship, only this time it wasn't as crazy. Oh, my depression was still there and her anxiety was still very much present, but for the first time in a long while, we are able to enjoy one another's company. It was decided fairly quickly that Shannon would move to Ottawa.

Although I certainly wasn't forgiven for my horrible and cowardly decision of fleeing while she was at work, we both figured it was something we could work through. A love that survives turmoil like this has to mean something. It just has to.

We decided that maybe our problem was that we moved in together too soon. So we decided to back things up a little, and start from scratch.

I was enlisted with the task of finding her an apartment while she headed back to pack her things.

The process took about a month. During that month, the band and I practised every single day and tried to make ourselves Ottawa ready. Coming from a small town, we knew that we would have a lot of competition in the big city and wanted to make an impression. I had visited Ottawa many times, since my older brother went to University there, but Shannon had never been prior. I had moved to Ottawa, or rather, ran away to Ottawa, for a chance at music. She had moved to Ottawa for a chance at me.

I found her a very chic apartment right in the centre of the city, which was only a few blocks from where me and the members of Caparosa, as we were called, were staying. She moved in, and we started the Ottawa chapter of our insanity.

I had completely and utterly given up on school. I figured I was destined to make it on my own as a writer and musician, and I was certainly in the right city for such. There were opportunities every which way. Caparosa started gigging around town, playing a style of acoustic inspired grunge rock. This made me incredibly happy. For the first time in many years, it felt as though I had finally figured out what I was meant to do. I was meant to be poor, working a menial, low-paying job all the while playing music.

I worked terrible, terrible jobs. I lasted about three days as a telemarketer before I was fired. I worked selling printer cartridges. I worked as a construction labourer. I worked the overnight shift at an Internet Café. My longest lasting job was as a grill cook. I basically got to barbecue for eight hours a day, which was fine for me. In my mind, I was just paying the bills until Caparosa made it big.

Shannon had transferred from her old retail job and continued to do that to pay the bills. We weren't happy, but it was as close to it as either of us had been since we had met. Shannon eventually became friends with the other members of Caparosa, who initially feared and despised her. The name 'Yoko' came up quite often during band practise. Looking back now, the guys in my band were pretty huge dicks. That was our life. I was working crap jobs and trying to make it in the music world and

Shannon was working a crap job and just trying to make it in her own mind. A simple change of scenery isn't enough to make an anxiety disorder go away. But for at least the first year, she was doing better than I had ever known her to be.

About a year after we moved to Ottawa, we noticed that I was spending a lot more time at her apartment than I was at my own and realized that, financially, it made sense for us to move in together. Again. At least this time we had given our relationship some time to grow. Things would be different this time. We really hoped that things would be different this time. Please, let things be different this time.

19

THE FINAL INSANITY

We found a perfect apartment. It was in the same neighbourhood that she was already living in. It was a two-bedroom and I was permitted to make the extra bedroom into a music room. It was covered in posters, littered with CD's and had guitars and amps strewn all over the place. We had a front balcony and a back porch and a backyard with a barbecue. It was perfect.

I lasted about a year as a grill cook before I couldn't take any more. I always had money missing on my paychecks, was often not given a break for six hours at a time and had to work with the scorching heat of the grill in front of me and the scorching heat of the rotisserie behind me. A few months before we moved back in together, I started a job in a warehouse. It was meant to be a temporary job, until something better came along. I was also writing music reviews for some online publications and doing some print work for local music rags on the local music scene, in addition to freelancing for a national news service writing a weekly opinion column, as well as three reviews per week. None of my writing jobs paid enough to pay the bills, so I had to do something else in the meantime. I took the gig at the warehouse, seeing it as a temporary solution to our money problems.

I, however, was unaware that working in a warehouse is quite similar to working in a prison. Well, at least the one I worked in. It was a company that built office supplies and I was in charge of building cubicle panels. The job itself sucked, but that wasn't what got to me. It was the people who worked there. The workforce seemed to be made up of aging high school bullies and convicted felons.

The good thing about it was that it was a Monday to Friday job, during the day, which is extremely hard to find as an unskilled labourer. The bad thing about it was every single other thing. The work was repetitive and monotonous, there was no room for creativity, and certainly no room for error. Every single thing you did was analyzed down to the finest detail and any imperfections caused a great scene. And my boss was a dick. And his boss was a dick. And every single employee was a dick.

It was sort of like being in high school again, but this time, I couldn't just leave, since I was being paid. I was once duct-taped inside the bathroom. My tools were often left covered in spit. I was mercilessly made fun of, from the start of the day to the very end. Every single day.

Things never got physical, since no one wanted to get fired, but the other employees did everything in their power to make me feel unwelcome. It was obvious that I didn't belong there. I was a white-collar mind stuck in a blue collar job. History has shown us that people do not like what they don't understand. And I was certainly misunderstood.

I stuck it out. The pay was decent and it was full-time work. After all the crap jobs I had had before this, I knew there wasn't anything else out there for me. So I worked on my writing, gathered my tiny weekly writing pay checks and hoped that soon enough, something would give, and I would be able to quit. That didn't happen.

My ability to handle these adverse daily situations was diminishing greatly. Spending eight hours a day getting made fun of by a bunch of newly released criminals got to me. I started drinking heavily. It became the only thing that could get me through the shit that was my daily life.

I was depressed, but it was a new kind of depression. It wasn't the same one I felt before. It was a much more hopeless depression. I didn't see the point in cutting myself or taking a few too many pills. If I was going to do something, it was going to be drastic. I started thinking of laying down in front of an oncoming train.

It became my obsession. I investigated train routes and got to know where the best place would be to commit the final deed. I had done my research. I even did some dry runs and laid down on some tracks to get a sense of what it would feel like. Much of the reason that I was still alive was that I was terrified of the physical pain that goes along with a suicide attempt. Since I didn't have access to a gun, I figured laying in front of a train to be the least painful and most successful way.

It would be painful, yes, but the pain would only last a fraction of a second. After that, you would be dead. At peace. Gone.

I told Shannon that I was thinking these horrible things. She did her best.

It didn't help things that Shannon's anxiety had morphed itself into something completely new. She was now developing obsessive compulsive traits, which made her daily life much more difficult than it already had been. We tried to get her help too. But the help that was available, in our very limited budget, was a giant waste of time. She had one therapist who believed only in New Age remedies and multiple others that weren't worth the paper that their degrees were printed on. Once we were finally able to get her in to see a psychiatrist, there was an ominous sign on the door. It read: "Dr. X is now only accepting female patients."

After a few fairly unproductive sessions, we found out through the news media that this psychiatrist had been arrested for coercing his male patients into sexual acts and was now in prison.

I was seeing a medical doctor at the time who was prescribing me antidepressants but after many months, I knew that they weren't going to do me any good. It wasn't a missed connection between the neurons in my brain. It was a hatred of my life, and a desire for death.

So we were both left to our own devices.

About eleven months after we had moved in together and I started working in the warehouse, things became completely intolerable for me. At least, by this point, I realized when I was losing control of my mind.

After a sleepless night of deep anxiety and psychotic depression, my plan of taking my own life came all too close to coming true. I was at the point of wanting to make the trip to the train track, lying there peacefully, closing my eyes, counting down from one hundred and just waiting for the pain to stop.

That day Shannon went with me to see my doctor. She told me not to lie to him; to tell him what I had been telling her. So I did. He had me sent to the emergency department of the hospital.

I was admitted on a Form 1. It was a form written by the psychiatrist in the emergency room that stated that I needed to be admitted to hospital for assessment for at least 72 hours because I was at great risk of harming myself.

I had to spend the night in one of the ER beds and was brought to the psych ward in the morning.

This psychiatric hospitalization was nowhere near as eventful as the last. I was a model patient. I wanted to be better. I was fucking sick of feeling this way, and wanted it to end. I wanted to finally understand what was wrong with me. Once the 72 hours were up, I convinced my psychiatrist that I wasn't going to run away. I wanted to be there. I needed to be there. So, he gave me my clothes back.

It's an interesting concept. They take someone in who is extremely depressed and suicidal, take away all his clothes and force him to wear hospital gowns for the first three days, the rationale being that it is a lot harder to escape when wearing only hospital gowns. The reality is that it only makes you feel more insane than you already are. This approach is falling fast as clinicians begin to have a more comprehensive understanding of the dehumanizing effect of being locked up in a psychiatric ward and being Robbed of everything that makes you a unique person.

The only good part of that job that had destroyed my sense of self was that they offered disability pay. I was able to go into hospital and know that Shannon wouldn't be left paying the rent and bills on her own. Which was a good thing, because I wound end up staying there for quite some time.

20

CONVERSATIONS IN PSYCHIATRY

I got to witness a whole new side of psychiatric care this time around. I wasn't psychotic, meaning I wasn't experiencing any hallucinations or delusions, so I was able to take in the entire experience. I sort of viewed it as my chance to have the best minds in psychiatry figure me out once and for all. Just give me a diagnosis, so I can tend to it and go about the rest of my life.

For the first part of my hospitalization, I was given a resident psychiatrist, as it was a teaching hospital. Before even taking my case history, he suggested electro-convulsive therapy, or ECT, what was formerly known as shock therapy.

When he told me that, I told him to leave my room. I spent the next several hours just sobbing uncontrollably. It had come to the point that I was crazy enough that a doctor was telling me that I needed to be shocked back into sanity. It was a harsh reality. I knew I was fucked up, but I wasn't willing to let anyone shock my brain back into the real world.

I told this doctor the next day that I would not consent to that, so he instead started a strict regimen of a ridiculous amount of drugs. Within two weeks of being there, I was on 30 pills a day. I only got worse.

After about a month of my condition going from very bad, to much, much worse, his superior took over my case. I was extremely thankful. I felt as though my problems were not textbook and that they couldn't be solved by a recent graduate from medical school. I was very happy to be working with this new doctor, who was the chief of psychiatry at the hospital.

His first order of business upon taking on my case was to discontinue half of the medications I was on. He didn't see any need to over medicate me, knowing that it likely wasn't a chemical problem. It was a life problem. He proceeded to do something that I had never seen a psychiatrist do; he used his words, instead of a prescription pad.

He gave me one hour sessions, every few days. I was permitted to talk about whatever I wanted. I came to each meeting with a notepad filled with questions, comments and concerns as well as my mood diary. I kept a very detailed and organized record of my moods, in the hopes that it would help the psychiatrist figure me out. I finally had someone who seemed to be on my side, someone who understood that perhaps my problems were deeper than a simple chemical imbalance.

I told him everything. Everything that had happened from childhood up until my incarceration at the asylum. He listened. And he cared. Which are the two most important things than anyone in a counselling profession should learn before any theory is ever applied.

One thing that I remember clear to this day is his response to the question of 'do you think I have bipolar disorder?'

His answer was, 'Do you?'

This was the perfect answer to the question that I had seeking to have answered for so many years. It gave me the power to use my own deductions to figure myself out. As he later explained, I am the one who knows myself best. Therefore, I am the most qualified to make a diagnosis. He knew that I had done my research and that I was very aware of all the different types of psychiatric illnesses and their symptoms.

So, my answer was 'no.'

I didn't think I had bipolar. I thought that I made some big mistakes when I was younger, did far too many drugs which took away my ability to sleep and caused me to become psychotic. The depression that followed was a direct reaction to the confusion of losing one's mind. And the current depression I was in could be mostly explained by my dismal life circumstances; working a dead-end job, having flunked out of college twice, living in a very stressful relationship. However, I didn't think I was 'normal' by any stretch of the imagination. I knew that I was probably more aware and in tune with my feelings than most people, which might have contributed to some of my difficulties. All in all, I thought I was an eccentric and creative guy who had a few run-ins with bad luck that ended with terrible consequences. But I did not think I had bipolar. And I did not think I had schizophrenia. I was just a guy with some bad luck who was battling some severe clinical depression and anxiety. And in all honesty, who isn't battling depression and anxiety?

While I was in the hospital, I spent most of my time reading. I would ask my psychiatrist to get me literature on different mental illnesses and their treatments, and my passion started growing. I slowly started to discover that knowledge is power. I also started to think that 'hey, I could do what he's doing.'

I told the treatment team that maybe I wanted to work with others who had experienced mental illness. Although they didn't tell me not to, they certainly didn't encourage me. And that makes sense. You need to be able to help yourself before you can help anyone else. But the road had begun. Helping others, that was the key to happiness. I had finally figured it out.

I still loved writing and wasn't about to abandon my writing career, but the idea of helping other people just seemed to make so much sense. Writing is my first love. Sometimes, the things you write can help other people a great deal. Being face to face with someone who is dealing with severe emotional problems and helping them to find a solution seemed like an extremely appealing plan. But since I was still an inpatient in a highly secured psychiatric hospital, I knew I had a tall order ahead of me before I could get to the other side of the desk.

I had hope, though. And hope is all you need.

I started my informal training by trying to figure out what other patients on the ward were suffering from, just by observing them. There were a lot of sick people there, all suffering from different ailments. There was one older man who would just dial random telephone numbers and yell gibberish at whoever answered. There was another young guy who just stood at the door to his room and stared a dark and vicious stare, straight-ahead, all day long.

We all had to share rooms on this ward. Four to a room. I was able to make one friend out of my endlessly circulating list of roommates over the six weeks. A guy named Michel was on the bed next to me. He was one of the kindest people I had ever met, and he was horribly depressed, just as I was. We learned a lot from each other. First off, we didn't learn many healthy things from one another. We compared and contrasted methods of suicide. He was planning on walking in front of a bus. I countered with, "But there's a huge chance that it wouldn't kill you and would just maim you for life."

"Fuck, I never even considered that," he said.

I told him of my train track plan, and he seemed to agree that it just might be the way to go. As we got to know one another, we talked about everything under the sun. Michel had a severe drinking problem, which only served to worsen his depression. He wouldn't drink with other people either. Would never drink in a bar. He would just sit in a dark room and drink and 'talk to the bottle.'

I did my best to help Michel with my limited knowledge. He wasn't really the reading type, so I shared much of what I had learned about depression with him. If he ever wanted to know something in particular, I would go to the library and search the Internet for him. We sort of became a team.

I didn't tell him of my past psychiatric hospitalization, probably because I didn't really tell anyone about it. But at that moment in time, we were very similar. Although he was much older than me, we were both beaten down by the realities of life and were constantly contemplating suicide. We would share stories about our doctors or about which nurses we found to be incompetent. There's a lot of time to kill when you're in a psych hospital, so it was nice to have someone I could identify with. Many of the other people on the ward were far beyond being able to hold a conversation, so I did most of my talking with Michel.

Our roommates would come and go, but we were always there. I was there for six weeks, and he would have been there much longer as he was there when I was admitted and still hadn't left by the time I had. I don't know what happened to him. The optimist in me likes to believe that he conquered his demons, but the realist in me knows the dangers of combining alcohol and depression. It can be a lethal combination. A great number of both attempted and completed suicides involve alcohol, which makes sense. It dulls the senses, lessens your inhibitions and just generally makes it easier to do the deed.

My train track plan always involved a copious amount of alcohol. No sober person could ever wilfully lie in front of an oncoming train. Even being completely wasted out of one's mind likely wouldn't make it a whole lot easier.

Looking back now, I think my conversations with Michel were what got me interested in counselling in the first place. I sort of had a knack for it; people listened to me and appreciated what I had to say. And I have always been an extremely non-confrontational person, which is appealing for anyone sitting across from you, telling you their problems.

I was still a very long way away from ever counselling someone in a professional setting. The first step was probably to get myself out of psychiatric custody.

My thrice weekly meetings with my psychiatrist got more and more intense as we started talking about discharge. There were still a few things that I desperately needed to figure out. Although I loved her deeply, I felt as though the past was enough proof to show that Shannon and I living together, or being together was a bad idea. It just isn't that easy. When two people have become so entrenched in each other's lives, it becomes difficult to see where one begins and one ends, especially two people who had gone through such psychological trauma together.

Details aside, I decided that at least not living with Shannon was the best option for my mental health at the moment. Putting that plan into action, however, was not going to be easy.

I was faced with a difficult task, and one that is especially difficult to tackle in a depressed state. On a pass from the hospital one afternoon, I went to the tattoo parlour and got the Edvard Munch painting *The Scream* tattooed on my right forearm. It was the only thing that could represent the inner turmoil that I was experiencing.

My psychiatrist basically decided that I was as good as I was going to get. I was sent off after six weeks with a bunch of pills and a note telling me to go straight to the emergency room if the thoughts of suicide became unbearable again.

21

OH, SO ELUSIVE

After much painful and extremely emotional conversation, it was decided that Shannon and I would move into separate apartments, but temporarily stay together as a couple. It was sort of a compromise on the whole breaking up completely thing. There was one slight problem: neither of us were exactly raking in the money. She was still working in retail and I was surviving off of disability cheques from my horrible job. So, we found the two cheapest apartments around. I moved into a bachelor apartment right in the center of the crack dealers and the street-walkers, and Shannon moved into a one-bedroom, just a few blocks away also, in the worst neighbourhood in town.

We rented a big moving van, and with the help of a few friends got all of our stuff to our respective new apartments by mid-afternoon. I locked up my new place and we all went over to Shannon's new place, since it was bigger, for beer and pizza. I walked back to my new home to crash before midnight sometime. It was only a few minute walk which was nice.

I got into my apartment and noticed that the door to my balcony was wide open. I started panicking. I turned on all the lights. My fridge was open, my boxes were strewn all over the place. It was extremely difficult to tell what was missing since I had literally just moved in and everything was scattered around the room in no particular order.

But there were definitely a few things missing. Some electronics, and all the moving-in beer from the fridge. It really wasn't what was stolen; it was the fact that someone had been in my home. On the first fucking night. Someone had broken into my house on the first fucking night.

I called back to Shannon's house and she and our mutual friend Larry came right over. We all surveyed the situation and all signs pointed to my immediate next door neighbour who had briefly visited during the move-in.

He had long, mangled hair and a big goatee, and probably topped out around six-foot-two, and he'd come over to welcome me to the neighbourhood. He seemed friendly enough, so we invited him in for a beer since we were done moving me in. We all sat on the gorgeous balcony, which was the one nice feature of this place, and smoked cigarettes. At one point during our conversation, he took out his cigarettes and a rock of crack cocaine slipped out. He justified it with the fact that it was his girlfriend's. She was paranoid and didn't want to keep her crack on her so he held it for her. But he didn't do the stuff himself, of course.

Not being one to judge others for their afflictions, I thought barely anything of it. I certainly didn't know that he was there scoping out my things with the plan of stealing them later, probably to sell for money to buy more crack cocaine. For his, err, girlfriend.

His name was Kirk and he became another completely incomprehensible addition to my already mangled life.

We phoned the police and they arrived promptly. We had left the door to the balcony as it was, half ajar. Just by looking at the other balconies, it was simple to tell that there was only one that would be accessible to mine. It was Kirk's, right next door. The police knocked on his door. Banged on his door. Nothing. They stood on my balcony and shone an extremely powerful spotlight directly in his living room. I could hear him through the walls before the police arrived. I knew he was in there. This would come to be Kirk's little trick that he would have to use nearly every weekend during the time that I lived next door to him.

The police took my statement and a list of everything that was missing. They agreed that it was most likely Kirk, especially after I told them that he was there in the afternoon and was an obvious crack user. I told the cop that it was the first time I had ever seen crack. He responded with 'now that you've moved in here, it won't be the last.'

Wonderful.

They couldn't really do a whole lot, for some reason. The neighbour on the other side had come over during the panic to tell us about Kirk. He said that he was a very weird guy. He could be violent. He smokes crack. He gets involved with the police a lot. I can basically guarantee you that this was him that broke into your apartment. There still wasn't anything else the police could do. I was told to contact them if he threatened me or something.

Wonderful.

So I was left in my new apartment in the ghetto, knowing that my neighbour, sleeping fifteen feet away, was a violent crack user who had just broken into my apartment. What a great way to start my path towards complete mental recovery.

I became friends with the other neighbour, Mark. He was a very nice, but very peculiar individual. He obviously suffered from a severe anxiety disorder. Through Mark, I had heard that Kirk was denying that he broke into my house and that he was going to stop by to explain himself.

One night, the rap at the door. I figured that I couldn't avoid this forever, so I might as well not start now, and opened the door. It was Kirk, with a huge smile on his face and two beers. I allowed him to come in and he started talking about this 'rumour' that he broke into my apartment. Well, that was certainly not the case, but he might know who did do it.

I knew this was a load of shit. Seeing this guy face to face again, now with the new knowledge of his psychopathy, I had no intention of trying to challenge him in any respect. I decided to accept the fact that I lost a few things. Maybe if I'm nice to this guy, he won't kill me in my sleep. And he was unavoidable too. Our balconies were basically connected, and I spent as much time as possible on my balcony. The apartments weren't very big, so getting out on the balcony, no matter the temperature, was always an appealing idea.

I settled in with the fact that my neighbour was a crack smoking criminal who had broken into my house. I would now engage in polite conversation on our mutual balconies as the leaves changed in the fall months.

Trouble seemed to follow him wherever he went; it made sense, considering the crowd he hung out with. One of his best friends, and perhaps the 'girlfriend' he had spoken of previously, was a prostitute who worked in the area. I'm not entirely sure what their relationship entailed. I'm sure he wasn't her pimp, as he would have assuredly bragged about that at some point. He could just have been a customer, but she seemed to spend a lot of time over there. Nearly every weekend, and a few nights during the week. And when she was around, the police never seemed to be far behind.

I almost became immune to the sound of 'Kirk! We know you're in there. Open the door!' But Kirk would never make a peep. Everyone knew he was in there, but he knew his rights. If they didn't have a warrant, then they couldn't enter his house. So long as he didn't answer the door, he wouldn't get in trouble.

It was infuriating for me since I so badly wanted to see him punished for something, but he knew how to avoid getting caught. I never knew the entire scope of what he was involved with criminally, but I certainly know that crack cocaine, prostitution and B&Es were high up on the list. Any given weekend, you wouldn't be able to guess why the police were banging on his door.

One night, Kirk was on his balcony and I was on mine and he decided to bring up the supposed break and enter on my home, insisting that he had nothing to do with. After getting to know him a little, I was no longer as afraid as I initially was. I should have been…but I wasn't.

I called him on it and said it was a bullshit story and that he knew it. "I know it was you who broke into my fucking apartment."

He didn't take kindly to this. He got intensely angry. I could see the blood rushing through his eyes. He swore at me up and down and threatened every possible threat. We were no longer friendly neighbours.

A completely unrelated incident would be the next blow to this boiling pot of an existence between Kirk, Mark and I. Mark, apparently not being the nice guy that I originally pegged him for, was caught beating his girlfriend in the apartment lobby by the security cameras. All the tenants had access to the security footage on their TV's and Kirk often had it on, waiting for people since he didn't have a phone to access his buzzer, and so happened to be watching when that happened.

Mark was taken away by police and charged. He spent a night in jail. Kirk apparently forgot momentarily that he hated me and shared the news of what he had seen on the security camera, and also of what he planned on putting Mark through when he was released from jail. It's interesting how criminals have codes. Kirk would steal just about anything from anyone, but if you hit a woman, he takes the situation into his own hands.

Mark was only out of jail a few hours when he ran into Kirk at the end of our street, having just gotten off the city bus. Kirk waited until the bus pulled away, and then unleashed a massive beating on Mark, cussing at him, spitting on him and explaining thoroughly what this beating was for. He kicked him in the face, arms, back, legs. Everywhere. No part of his body was spared.

To put it lightly, this was a messed up situation that I was literally in the middle of. My one psychotic neighbour had just beaten the living hell out of my apparently other deadbeat neighbour. And now we were all expected to live in harmony, basically, together, separated only by a few thin walls. And if we're on our balconies, separated by barely anything at all.

Mark ended up calling the police and reporting Kirk for the assault. Of course, he didn't take into account that Kirk was apparently impossible to apprehend. The police showed up at his door, announced why they were there, and commanded him to open the door. This would happen every few hours for at least a couple of days.

Kirk knew what was up. One day I got home from the store and saw that Mark's door had been spray-painted with the words 'Wife Beating Rat Piece of Shit Lives Here.'

The cops were there again, and again, nothing happened.

A woman-beater and a rat are, next to being a pedophile, two of the worst things you can be in prison mentality. Mark had made his chances much more slim by calling the police on Kirk. Kirk now had a vendetta against him.

I talked to Mark sometimes when were on our balconies. I figured that everyone should at least have the chance to explain themselves. He explained that he had had way too much to drink, and he doesn't even remember hitting her. He obviously felt horrible. It was difficult to tell whether this was the first time this had happened or if it was a continuing occurrence.

Whether it was good or not, I do not know, but the two of them eventually continued seeing one another. She had somehow forgiven him for his violent indiscretion, but the charges were still pending - there was nothing they could do about that. And since they were legally prohibited from being together, they had to keep their relationship a secret. It was an extremely messed up situation.

Kirk caught me talking to Mark on the balcony one day and that was it. I was now as bad as Mark was in Kirk's eyes. My life became increasingly more bizarre as Kirk's behaviour continued to escalate in a psychotic direction. I think by then he was smoking crack more regularly, and it showed in everything he did.

I would often get long and threatening messages left on my voicemail. They would ramble and not really be all that coherent. But the general theme was that I was to watch my back. He would be as loud as humanly possible in his apartment when he knew I was home. It sometimes felt and sounded as if he was hitting my wall with a sledgehammer. The superintendent would come and bang on his door but he would always pretend to not be there, and he would eventually give up. It's like he had nothing better to do than to try and torment me at every opportunity.

These stressful times did nothing to help my relationship with Shannon. I suppose we were still trying to be boyfriend and girlfriend, but it was apparent that it wasn't working. Shannon had in fact become very close friends with one of my old tormentors from work while I was in the hospital. As I despised him to his very core for what he put me through, I did not gladly accept their relationship.

Shannon and I began to act more and more volatile towards each other and it was eventually decided that we just needed to stop. I would go on to take it to a new level, and move out of the city. I needed to get away from her, I needed to get away from Kirk, I just needed to get away from my life.

Around then, I had begun talking online to a girl I used to know. Within a very short amount of time, I decided to make another horrible decision. I decided to move six hundred kilometres away into the house of a girl I barely knew, at least temporarily solving the Shannon situation, and permanently solving the Kirk situation.

The girl managed a music store and had the same exact musical interests as I. I now know that you should never base an entire relationship simply along a mutual basis of music. It turned out that we didn't have much else in common. And the house, which we shared with a mid-thirties dreadlocked turbo hippy, was once again located in a pretty shitty part of town. I ended up getting jumped outside of our apartment and had my nose broken as well as my thumb.

To top all of this off, the girl I had moved in with had checked herself into the local psychiatric ward for an unspecified anxiety, depression and eating disorder combination shortly after I had moved in. It was too much. I just couldn't fucking take it anymore. But for the first time, I didn't think about suicide.

It was that day that I decided I couldn't stop the chaos on my own anymore. I had to take the plunge and move back home with my parents for a while. Chaos just seemed to be following me everywhere I went. There was no escaping from it. But I knew my parents' home, located in quiet suburbia would be a good place to finally get my thoughts together.

I had been staying in fairly close contact with my parents by telephone during these turbulent times. They had often offered the option of moving back home, but I guess I had too much pride. They were also sick of the insanity that seemed to follow me everywhere I went, and gladly welcomed me home.

22

THE ROAD BACK HOME

My parents' support was always unwavering. They knew me very well. After all, they had raised me. They knew the potential I had. And they knew that I could beat the torment that had been following me around every step I took. They did everything they could, and I will always be extremely grateful to them for that.

They offered me the downstairs of their suburban house in the city, equipped with a bedroom, living room and bathroom. They also set me up with a therapist. I don't know how they found her, but she ended up being the absolute perfect fit.

Her name was Teresa and she specialized in all different sorts of mental ailments. She worked with relationship problems, eating disorders, drug addiction, depression, anxiety and everything in the middle. She certainly seemed adequately trained to take on my mountain of troubles.

As I have explained previously, there is a certain way of being with another person that is paramount to any successful therapy. If the client doesn't feel at ease with the therapist, then it will be difficult to accomplish anything meaningful. Teresa had an excellent and intriguing personality. She was quite eccentric, which helped me to trust her. I considered myself to be quite the eccentric as well, so I felt we were somehow connected by that. We both shared a unique view of the world, but she had the pieces of paper on the wall to back up her theories.

My first few sessions were extremely difficult. I just had so much history that needed to be let out in order for her to get a full and complete understanding of me. But I was wholeheartedly dedicated to making this work. I viewed this as my last attempt at gaining some insight into an uncontrollable mind, and I had complete confidence that she would be the one who could finally help me achieve this goal.

She was genuinely interested in my story, which made it much easier to share personal and often painful details of the things that I had been through. Once she felt as though she had a fair enough idea of my past, we immediately began to work on my present.

I had the issues of my hospitalizations and what they meant. I still had major issues with Shannon, our relationship still being incredibly complex, but now from far away. I also had the very fresh issues of dealing with the few month girlfriend who ended up in the psychiatric hospital and who had developed a deep obsession for me.

She wrote me letters constantly, and each one would send me into an emotional whirlwind. And then Teresa told me that next time she sends a letter, just rip it up and throw it away. I couldn't control what she did, but I could control what I did in response to it. I just couldn't give her the chance to get to me. It seemed so simple, yet so complex. Why had I never thought of this before?

Teresa used a variety of simple yet beautiful techniques such as this while helping me sort out my problems. I would later understand during my own studies that she was using Cognitive Behavioural Therapy, Rational Emotive Therapy and Motivational Interviewing, the three main techniques that would become the cornerstone of my own counselling sessions years down the road.

CBT based interventions are now one of the most used and most respected forms of therapies for a wide-variety of emotional and behavioural problems. The basic concept is that one cannot change the event, but that one is in control of how to choose to react to the event. If you change the thinking, you change the feeling.

With this new knowledge and the practical training provided by Teresa, I was now able to apply the principles of CBT into my everyday thinking. The only thing I am in control of is my reaction. No matter what happens, I always have control over that.

Everything in my life began to be spun in a more positive light. Things just became easier. At first, I met with Teresa once a week. As I started to get better and better, my appointments decreased in frequency.

One day we got to talking about a career path for me. We talked about my fascination with mental illness. She gave me a few textbooks on abnormal psychology to look over. I devoured them. It was a true and real fascination. I talked about wanting to be a therapist and she agreed that it would be a good idea. She knew that with my story, and my ability to keenly identify with people from all aspects of life, that I would one day make a great therapist.

Our visits went down to about once a month. I had succeeded in making a healthy group of friends for once. I became involved in an environmental festival and organized the day long event's music. Through this experience, I met a great deal of wonderful, down to earth people. One friend, Kevin, was actually the one who convinced me to bring my music back out to the people.

I had played some acoustic guitar around a campfire one night and I guess had impressed Kevin. He was a hipster, very aware of every band you have never heard of. He vowed to help me get my music out there. With Kevin as my manager, I began playing solo shows around town and even played at the festival that we were organizing.

Life was starting to feel good again. Well, not again. For the first time, life was starting to feel good.

My relationship with Shannon had triumphed and we had morphed into excellent friends. We were both now dating other people and were even able to talk to one another about it. She was happy that she could hear in my voice that I was finally enjoying life.

I started a band, for the first time in several years. I had a wonderful group of extremely caring friends. Some were getting married, some were finishing their degrees, some were political activists, some were environmentalists and many of them were musicians or music junkies.

None of them were criminals. None of them were drug addicts or alcoholics. It was the perfect time and the perfect people to be around to collect one's sanity.

I decided to pursue my dream of counselling people with mental illnesses and enrolled in the Mental Health and Addictions counselling program. It felt great to be back in school, in the right frame of mind for once. I easily got A Honours in all of my courses. It was a breeze because everything that was being taught was just so incredibly interesting to me. I was finally able to learn what all the people who had been trying to help me for years had learned. I was mesmerized and I immediately excelled.

There were courses in trauma counselling, psychology, substance abuse, sociology, crisis intervention, group therapy techniques, cognitive behavioural therapy and everything in between. It was truly an amazing program and one that perfectly suited my interests. I became a close ally with the program coordinator, as I was a bit older and I guess more mature than the other students. He, along with another professor, became excellent aids in my understanding of mental health treatment. They both had varied backgrounds in crisis counselling, trauma counselling, marriage counselling and substance abuse counselling, and they seemed to enjoy every single minute of it. I knew that I had figured out exactly what I was meant for. There was no doubt in my mind. Helping people was what I was supposed to do.

I became even more involved in volunteer efforts. I started a Mental Health section in the school paper and wrote articles surrounding eating disorders, addiction on campus, schizophrenia and other topics, simply hoping to reduce the stigma surrounding the subject of mental illness. I also co-organized a charity concert series that raised money for the local food bank. During the years I was there, we were able to raise thousands of dollars for the food bank and the soup kitchen, while simultaneously creating a beautiful organization of like-minded musicians.

My friend Brody, the editor of the school paper, and I started organizing concerts all over the city. All of a sudden, all of these hidden and extremely talented musicians started appearing. We built something in those few years that I was there, and it continues to thrive now that I have left.

My band, Bohemian Cove, recorded an EP and the track *The Bombs are Here* ended up being featured as the track of the day on national radio. The large scale environmental festival went off without a hitch. We were raising money and raising awareness, all the while I was excelling at school. I was finally running on all cylinders. And it felt amazing.

The school years seemed to go by in a flash. It's amazing how time flies when you are having good, natural and wholesome fun.

But I had potential to fulfill now. I couldn't stay cooped up in a small town. I moved back to Ottawa to begin my career working as a Concurrent Disorders Counsellor in a long-term treatment centre for clients with mental health issues who were recently released from prison and are also battling major life-threatening addictions. I felt immediately at home working with this class of people, who are considered difficult to treat. It is serving as a great foundation to continue working towards my Masters Degree in Social Work, with the eventual goal of working in private practise, and continuing with my writing and music career.

I found my passion. It feels right working with the mentally ill, the addicted and the down-trodden, the lonely and the hopeless, the afflicted and the infected. I developed a deep compassion for my fellow human over the years, which comes across in my dealings with clients. And although they don't necessarily know where I've been, they always know that I am there for them, in that moment, in their despair.

And that, above all, I understand.

Completely In Blue:
The Songs Behind The Words

Bohemian Cove

If you have read the book, you can surely tell that music has always been and continues to be a major influence in my life. A few months before publishing the book, I decided to go into the studio to record some of the songs that were mentioned in the book. Some of these songs were written during the flowery highs of psychotic mania and some in the desperate lows of depression.

For the five song musical accompaniment to ***Completely in Blue***, please visit www.completelyinblue.bandcamp.com.

Kindest regards,
Chris Curry

11165875R00107

Made in the USA
Charleston, SC
03 February 2012